APPRECIATING
WINE

PHILLIP HILLS

Collins

Phillip Hills *is the founder of the Scotch Malt Whisky Society, through which he led the revolution in public understanding of malt whisky and created the market for specially bottled fine malts which all whisky companies now supply. He is the director of The Malt Masterclass, a company specialising in corporate tastings and classes. He is also the first (and only) holder since 1791 of a private licence to distil whisky, which he does for demonstration purposes using a copper pot-still.*

HarperCollins Publishers
Westerhill Rd, Bishopbriggs, Glasgow G64 2QT

www.collins.co.uk

First published 2004

© Phillip Hills 2004

Reprint 10 9 8 7 6 5 4 3 2 1 0

ISBN 0 00 710153 8

A catalogue record for this book is available from the British Library.

Printed and bound in Great Britain by Clays Ltd, St Ives plc

CONTENTS

INTRODUCTION

The idea behind this book can be stated very simply. It is that people drink wine because it tastes nice. If it was nasty, folk wouldn't drink it. The book is about the taste of wine. Appreciating wine is about knowing what flavours a good wine ought and ought not to have, and being able to assess a wine for the presence or absence of those flavours.

Biologically, wine has four functions: it quenches thirst because it consists for the most part of water; it is a food because it contains nutrients; it intoxicates because it contains ethyl alcohol, and it pleases the taste because it contains all sorts of interesting compounds. The first three purposes can be served in many other ways, most of them less troublesome and expensive than making wine. The flavour is what sets wine apart and justifies the trouble and expense.

We should perhaps make it clear at the outset that by 'wine', we mean wine fermented from the juice of the grape. Any fruit can be made into wine, so long as it has sugars available for fermentation. There are some delicious fruit wines, though none which can compare with the wine of the grape. There are also some perfectly foul so-called wines, though in fairness it must be admitted that some of the latter originate in grapes. It is the case, though, that there are no great wines which are made from anything other than grape juice.

Our judgements as to the flavour of a wine are fraught with uncertainty and difficulty. Grape-based wines have been around for a very long time and wine has accumulated a remarkable detritus of associations and values. When the sommelier produces a bottle of his best, it comes to table with a penumbra of associations which owes little to the status of the stuff as grub or to its being distant cousin to a glass of water. Nor is the fact of this being an expensive way of getting high a sufficient explanation of the sommelier's attitude. The reverence with which the cork is drawn is referable ultimately, via the values of an extended society, to the flavour which the wine is expected to exhibit. Not that the sommelier or anyone else can be expected to put this in words, for there are very few meaningful flavour terms in any European language. The transmission of opinion about what is good and what isn't concerning wine tends to be by precept rather than by means of a critical vocabulary. Learning about taste requires the acquisition of appropriate skills and people in the wine trade tend to serve an apprenticeship – apprenticeship being the form of education best suited to the transmission of non-verbal skills. The aim of this book is to suggest a way of getting to know what really matters about wine, by a means slightly shorter than serving a craft apprenticeship.

You can't get to know about how wine should taste by reading books, for very few books about wine even mention flavour. There are books about every conceivable aspect of the making and consuming of wine, but almost none about how they taste. There is little which would indicate to a visiting extraterrestrial why so many people go to so much trouble to coax a drink from the juice of a grape when there are so many easier ways by which humans may quench their thirst and get good and drunk in the process.

So wherein lies the difference between a fine wine and, say, a decent cider? How are we to discern it and how are we to express it? The difference certainly appears to reside in the flavour, for cider acts as food, drink and intoxicant in the same way as wine does, but most people do not choose to drink cider every day. The fact is that wines simply taste better than just about any other alcoholic liquor. Almost the only beverage whose flavour will measure up to good wine is the product of the fermentation of the barley malt. Ale, like wine, has a raw material of great chemical complexity which, when operated upon by yeast, yields a potation of great subtlety and delight. Just as we prefer wine to other drinks on account of its flavour, so a good wine differs from a bad one by tasting better. But when we seek to discriminate, we are faced with the problem of how we can be confident of our judgement and how we can express it in such a way that other people will understand what we say.

Taking the first of these: it will help if we can be quite certain that good and bad wines really are quite different, and that we can tell the difference with a degree of assurance and objectivity sufficient to yield us, if not certainty, at least a degree of comfort. This is a bit like one of Wittgenstein's descriptions of definitions: they are fine so long as you stay close to the core meaning, but as soon as you stray from the centre, they start to look dodgy. In any respectable restaurant in Paris there will be a pretty close consensus as to what is and isn't good wine. There may be minor disagreements, about matters such as which are the very best wines, which are the best vintages, which wines age best, and the like, but not radical differences about what's a decent wine. Certainly our French connoisseurs would look down on a woman I know, who drinks Lambrusco because she likes it. This lady is no different from a great many other ladies of her age and class in preferring Lambrusco. What perhaps is unusual is that her independence of mind is allied to a very powerful intellect and a first-rate education. She has the esteem of a wide and cultured society, she is not poor, nor does she lack the acquaintance of persons expert in fine wines, in whose company she has downed a lot of the expensive stuff. She still likes to drink Lambrusco. It would be a brave man who taxed her with lack of discrimination and objectivity.

If it were just the odd individual, the problem could be ignored. But consider this: I once, as an experiment, served an unusual wine at a dinner party. I bought from a reputable wine merchant a quantity of an oxidised sweet white wine, made from vines of great antiquity. I mixed this wine with as much honey of the first quality as it would hold. I brought a bucket of seawater from a remote part of the coast, where the sea is free from effluents and pollution. I mixed the honeyed wine with the seawater in a proportion of one to two and served it to my guests. You can imagine the response: gagging and nausea and accusations of poison. One poor chap, who had downed a great draught, actually fled to the loo, where he threw up. When the fuss had died down, everyone wanted to know what was going on. I explained that what I had just served was wine of a sort and condition as close as I could make it – and I had no reason to suppose that was not pretty close – to the sort of drink which some of the greatest connoisseurs in the world had drunk for several centuries: certainly for much longer than there has been agreement as to what today constitutes decent wine. I refer, of course, to the wines which Roman senators served at their dinner tables and which people such as Pliny and Strabo wrote books about. For that is the case: in ancient Rome, a civilisation which lasted, even if you don't count Constantinople, for well over half a millennium, people who knew good wine drank sweet stuff mixed with seawater.

If the comparison with Roman customs seems a bit remote, we should perhaps consider something a little closer to home. By the early 19th Century, claret-drinking was a long-established custom of the British upper classes, many of whom were extremely knowledgeable and discerning drinkers. What is surprising to us today, is that they preferred to drink their red wines very cold, holding that it was in that condition that the wine was best able to exhibit its bouquet and flavour. They even had decanters known as marsupial jugs, from the pouch in which the ice was held. What is more, it appears that fine wines were commonly frozen, thawed and then frozen again, presumably because the process was thought to improve the flavour. To his credit, George Saintsbury described the former custom as barbarous and the latter as 'simply Bolshevist' (from *Notes on a Cellar Book*, Chapter 4).

It is difficult to resist the conclusion that our perception of what makes a good wine is largely determined by our society, and that quality in wine is not an objectively existing value. That's not too surprising, really, given that it's just drink at the end of the day, and the best drink is that which is most pleasing to our taste. Most people of any experience in matters of taste know that what pleases them now is not what pleased them as children. Tastes can be cultivated and we generally prefer a cultivated taste to an uninformed one. Appreciation has to do with the cultivation of taste and the exercise of judgement based on the values which come with cultivation.

To analyse the notion a little further: if we are to appreciate wine, we must know what tastes to look for in wine and how to look for them. These are the primary requirements of appreciating wine: there is a certain amount we can say about them. But much of what is known about wine is known by methods which bypass language. This is why the vocabulary of flavour is so poor compared with the vocabulary of, say, colour. So there are lots of secondary things we need to know about wines: factors which affect the flavour of the wine, even if we can't exactly specify the effect. That is why, as mentioned above, there are so many books about things which appear to have little relation to what really matters: the taste of the stuff. We shall touch on the secondary factors, knowing that they affect the flavour, even if we can't say exactly how. Once we have dealt with all that, we can look at a few wines.

Phillip Hills
2004

ON FLAVOUR

FLAVOUR

We began by saying that what matters about wine is that it tastes nice. Let us now refine the notion of taste. By 'taste' we commonly mean the pleasurable sensation we have on eating or drinking something. (Other meanings of 'taste' are derivative and not our present concern.) But what we normally call 'taste' is in fact a sensation made up of several quite different impressions, of which the main two are taste (in a stricter sense) and smell. For the purposes of this book, we shall use the term 'taste' to refer to the sensations which arise in our mouth and 'aroma' or 'bouquet' – or 'smell' - when we mean smell. The overall impression, which is made up of those two plus the other, minor sensations, we shall refer to as 'flavour'. We will now proceed to look at flavour, for an understanding of the mechanism of flavour makes the appreciation of wine a whole lot easier.

We are generally credited with five senses: sight, sound, touch, taste and smell. On examination, these turn out to involve responses to only three sorts of stimuli. When we see, we respond to electromagnetic radiation in a rather narrow waveband. Sound and touch are both perceptions of mechanical stimuli. Taste and smell are the sensations which we associate with chemical stimuli. Taste is the response to chemical stimulation of the receptor cells in the mouth and smell the same as regards the nose. When we eat or drink, the sensation which we usually describe as 'taste' is in fact made up of both taste and smell. If anyone doubts this, he or she need only recollect how having a common cold can alter the flavour of food and drink. If you have a bad cold, you can 'taste' very little. This is because an important component of flavour is the sensation of smell caused by odour components which pass in the air from the mouth via internal passages to the nose.

Chemoreception is, in evolutionary terms, by far the oldest of the senses. All living things are sensitive to the chemical makeup of their environment: in that respect, the Colonel's lady and the flu virus are sisters under the skin. Indeed critters which have any other senses at all are still a tiny minority of the living things inhabiting this planet: viruses, bacteria and unicellular organisms make up by far the largest part of the Earth's biomass. Such creatures inhabited the planet for some hundreds of millions of years before any of them got around to evolving the two touch senses or sight.

The primacy we accord to sight has caused us to downgrade other senses: where different senses provide conflicting information, we give primacy to that which we receive by sight. The only exception is as regards food and drink, and not always there: I have a friend whose daughter routinely disposes of food which has passed its sell-by date, despite her father's telling her that it smells fine and is therefore presumably OK. With few exceptions, smell is a reliable indicator of whether food is off – but few people in the developed world now prefer their sense of smell to what it says on the packet.

The primacy accorded to sight applies to wine tasting as it does to most other human activities, for the appearance of a wine undoubtedly affects how we perceive its flavour. Whether this is a good thing or not depends on your point of view. Most books about wine mention appearance as an important indicator of flavour, and the Commission Internationale de l'Eclairage went to the trouble of devising a system of standard wine colours, so evidently a lot of folk think the colour of wine is important. If the major premise of this book is correct, namely that the only thing that really matters about wine is its taste, then you might think there has to be a close correlation between the colour of a wine and its gustatory quality. But there is little evidence that a wine's colour provides us with any really reliable indication of how it will taste. With some wines, the colour can tell us something about the age of the wine – but not much, for the way the wine is made counts for far more than age in determining colour.

The colour of red wines derives from the grape pigmentation and different grapes are differently pigmented. A wine made from a Cabernet Sauvignon or a Shiraz grape will have a very deep-red colour until it is very old, while one made from Gamay or Pinot Noir grapes will usually – not always – be less-deep in colour. As they get older, red wines take on a brownish tinge. So brown in the red may indicate great age. But it may also be caused by oxidation or heating, so the colour unsupported by other circumstances cannot be taken as a reliable indicator of age. In a young, dry white wine, a very yellow colour may imply contamination – but it may also indicate that the wine has been matured in oak, or the colour may be the result of long maceration – so colour alone is not a reliable indicator of quality. In a sherry, a brown hue is a sign of the type of sherry, for sherries run the gamut of colour, from dead-pale Manzanilla to almost-black Pedro Ximenez. With Madeira, on the other hand, brown indicates heating and oxidation, both conditions which most wine makers go to great lengths to avoid but are desirable in Madeira, whose makers go a to a lot of trouble to achieve it.

Only where wines of the same sort but different ages are compared, and then only if they have been treated in exactly the same way, can the shade tell us anything useful. Otherwise, we have to discover so much about the causes of the colouration of that once we do, we shall have much more reliable indicators of the flavour of the wine than its colour alone can provide.

Mention is rarely made of the single most important way in which the appearance of a wine affects how people perceive its flavour. That is, the label on the bottle. For the great majority of drinkers, a wine bearing an expensive label will be perceived as being greatly superior in flavour to the same wine bearing a cheap label. This doesn't mean that all wine drinkers are excessively suggestible, merely that our perception of flavour has a large psychological component. This component is recognised in the organisation of serious comparative tastings, in which labels are always obscured.

TASTE

We taste by means of taste buds. About 10,000 of these are located in the mouth, most but not all of them on the tongue. The roughness of your tongue is caused by little growths called papillae, with which it is covered. There are three different sorts of these, and a minority contain epithelial cells which have receptor neurons which detect the chemical nature of whatever you put in your mouth. The receptor neurons are specialised so that they react to the presence of certain classes of chemical by sending impulses via one of the cranial nerves to the brain. The firing of the neurons appears to be caused by the neurons' binding with molecules of the substance tasted, or with proteins associated with them. There are glands in the taste buds which produce a protein thought to play a part in the process.

The tongue is the source of four main sorts of taste: sweet, sour, salt and bitter. All other components of flavour are caused by smell. (There may be minor exceptions to this, of which the principal is sensitivity to glutamates. The latter are certainly components of flavour, as is evidenced by their widespread use in Chinese cooking and the artificial flavouring industry, though whether we have specialised receptors for them is not yet established.) It has been suggested that we can distinguish two different sorts of sweetness and bitterness, but whether this is the case and if so, whether there are separate receptor mechanisms, has not been ascertained.

The neurons in the papillae at the front of the tongue are sensitive to sweetness, while bitterness is perceived on the rear central part of the tongue. Sourness we receive at the sides of the tongue and salt along the upper edge of the front. There is much individual variation in this: some people detect sourness inside the cheeks or behind the lips rather than on the tongue itself. The subjective sensations of sweetness and bitterness are very different, but their causal mechanisms are closely related, as are, indeed, the molecular structures of many sweet- and bitter-tasting compounds. Very small changes in the structure of some sweet-tasting compounds can turn them into bitter ones, and vice-versa. It is noticeable that sweet flavours can mask bitter and vice-versa.

Sweet flavours also mask sour ones, though the chemistry of their causes is very different. Wines, especially white wines, which are deficient in sugar, tend to taste sour, while wines which are high in acid become palatable given an adequate level of sugar. Hence the practice of adding sweetness to white wine which originated in northern Europe: beet or cane sugar in France and unfermented, sweet grape juice in Germany. (See the next chapter, Wine Flavours.) Sweetness and sourness are detected more rapidly than are the other tastes, and they do not linger as long as do bitter tastes. The taste of salt is rarely a consideration as regards wine – though presumably it was for the Romans, given their penchant for seawater.

People vary greatly in the sensitivity of their taste responses. Experiments have shown that some people are four or five times as sensitive as others. The variation is greatest as regards bitterness and least in respect of saltiness.

There are factors besides other tastes which affect our perception of flavour. The presence of alcohol enhances sweetness and some minor forms of bitterness, while it diminishes sourness, which is why wines of high alcoholic content tend to taste better than those of low. Temperature affects sensation as well: the bitterness of red wines increases as their temperature drops, which presumably is the reason (other than fashion) why reds are mostly taken at room temperature. Sparkling white wines benefit from the greater effervescence retained at low temperatures. Bitterness is more acceptable in white wines than it is in red, so heavily oaked Australian chardonnays are acceptable (to some people) despite the bitterness caused by the high level of tannins.

Some components of taste cause more than one sort of sensation. Ethyl alcohol itself is mildly sweet as well as the source of the burning sensation which we have when we take any strong liquor. Although wines usually do not contain enough alcohol to cause such sensations, some do, and even where it is not perceptible as a fiery feel, alcohol is the source of what some wine tasters describe as 'weight'. Tannins are not only bitter, they are astringent: a physical effect which is described below. Glucose tastes mildly sharp as well as sweet. Where some or all of these components are present, as they are in most wines, the small secondary sensations combined can have a significant effect in enhancing the primary flavours.

Our perception of tastes is affected both by what is going on in our bodies and what is going on outside them: by somatic and environmental factors, in formal language. We are all familiar with the depression of taste brought about by illness. Ditto the effect of previous experience on how we taste things. The red wine which we drank with the main course may have tasted just fine, but if we drink it with our dessert, it will taste very bitter indeed. It will, however, recover, if we persevere as far as the cheese. This is what the matching of wine with food is all about. It's not some mysterious thing which is apparent only to the connoisseur: it is simply that the taste of wine is grossly affected by the food we eat with it. It is almost all about sweetness and acidity and has very little to do with getting it right for the meat and the fish – the same wine will do very well for both fish and meat: just don't expect the crisp white which went just fine with the boeuf en croute to do for the bread-and-butter pudding, or the sweet Muscat which went with the charlotte malakoff to suit the Stilton.

Possibly the most important thing to take into account when tasting wine is the influence of a phenomenon called taste adaptation. This is the tendency for any taste to fade quickly if kept in contact with whatever we are tasting. We can all recall the frustration we suffered as children when the chocolates which were so blissful on Christmas morning had ceased to give pleasure by lunchtime. We have an inbuilt tendency to block any sensation which stays constant for any length of time. It is just as well, otherwise we would suffer from information overload. We can feel our socks when we put them on in the morning, but we don't want to have to be aware of our feet all day, for when we are driving the car or negotiating with a tiger, an awareness of the exact position of our toes serves no useful purpose. Indeed, such awareness would be distracting and an evolutionary disadvantage: we would crash the car or the tiger would get us. So we blank out sensation, tastes included. That said, there are ways of combating this and ways of turning it to our gustatory advantage, of which more in the section on tasting.

Some smells appear to make things taste sweet. When we detect the aroma of an ethyl ester (a compound created when ethyl alcohol reacts with an acid) , we tend to experience a sweet taste. It is not clear whether there is a direct causal connection or whether the impression is simply a result of the known association of such esters with sweet tastes. (Esters are typically to be found in fruits in association with sugars.)

Our age undoubtedly affects our taste sensations. We lose acuity as we get older, despite the fact that the receptor cells which detect flavour are constantly being replaced. Some people make up in experience what they lose by age: a good palate is, by and large, wasted on the young – but youth generally is, so it's no great surprise. Taste perception is influenced by the dental decay which goes with advancing years. There is an argument for having all your teeth out so as to negate the influence of caries in the detection of flavour. However desirable that may be for wine, it diminishes our appreciation of food and is not to be recommended. Our taste preferences change with age, too, and the loss of some acuteness may be recompensed by the discovery of pleasure in flavours which previously had been dismissed as noxious.

One's own actions can be regarded as in a sense an external factor. We can acquire a taste for flavours which, before the acquisition we found disagreeable. This rather mysterious process is a result of conscious intentional action and so extraneous to our natural perception of taste. How far this process can be carried is unclear, but it can go a surprisingly long way, though at its extremity, its outcome may be indistinguishable from madness.

Finally, one of the most important external factors: the influence of our society. Culturally-determined preferences are well known, viz. the Romans' taste for sweet wines with sea water, or the Victorians' preference for their red wines cold. It appears that our culture can actually determine our taste preferences and hence our actual taste sensations.

MOUTH SENSATIONS OTHER THAN TASTE

Taste is not the only feeling we have in our mouths. There are other sensations which contribute to the overall impression which we call flavour. These are classed together as mouth-feel and consist of the perception of temperature, astringency, body, prickling and burning.

The effect on our perception of flavour of the temperature at which a wine is served, has already been remarked in the case of red wines. Dry white wines are generally served cool: coolness seems to enhance our pleasure in drinking them, though why is not apparent, at least with still wines. The effervescence of sparkling wines is part of the pleasure and that pleasure is enhanced by coolness, for the gas which causes the effervescence is retained better when the wine is cool.

Astringency is probably the most important mouth-feel sensation. We are all familiar with it, though it is hard to say in what exactly it consists, apart from a feeling of dryness and a tendency for the mouth to pucker. It is not in fact a single sensation, but a group of responses to (mainly) phenolic compounds which are extracted from the seeds and skins of the grape. It can also be induced by sourness. In practice, astringency is experienced as part of the response to bitterness or sourness and is very difficult to dissociate from these tastes. Its mechanism appears to involve the precipitation of proteins which, coating the teeth, make them feel rough and, expelling water from the surface of the lining of the mouth, make it feel dry. It may be that constriction of the blood vessels in the lining of the mouth involved as well, and that this gives rise to the puckering feeling. Astringency is typically slow to take effect and lingers long after the cause is removed, hence its importance in the aftertaste of wines.

Body is rather a vague feeling, but one which is so commonly described by wine tasters that it cannot be ignored. Wines which have body usually have high sugar levels and low acidity. The presence of glycerol contributes to the body of a wine, which gives rise to the suspicion that it may have to do with viscosity. There is however no agreement as to its causes.

Prickling is the sensation which is produced by the bursting in the mouth of bubbles of carbon dioxide. It is more intense at lower temperatures and is sometimes associated with a burning sensation. It results from the stimulation of the endings of the trigeminal nerve. Most but not all drinkers find it pleasant.

The effect of ethyl alcohol on the mouth we have already mentioned. This is a burning sensation similar to that produced by some peppers and spices. It occurs when the alcohol content is over about 15%. Obviously, this excludes most wines. There is also a phenomenon known as sugar burn, which is experienced when drinking wines which have a very high sugar content, such as eisweins. Little is known about it.

SMELL

As a means of detecting the chemical makeup of our environment, the nose is a much more subtle instrument than the mouth. For a start, it is always open, whereas most people keep their mouth shut most of the time, and taste only if they put things in it. The nose, on the other hand, is always available to any passing breeze. We can detect odours even when we sleep: there are numerous examples of people being awakened by a smell, particularly of something burning.

The nose is a more sensitive instrument than the mouth, both in the range of stimuli which it can detect and in the concentrations at which it can detect them. If nose and mouth were radio receivers, the mouth would be set to get only four stations, and then only if the signal were strong. The nose, on the other hand, would pick up any signal over a vast bandwidth, and would be capable of detecting the faintest of signals. What is more, it would be able to discriminate between very faint signals as well as to discern combinations of signals. To get some idea of the order of the disparity between nose and mouth, we need only compare the instruments.

The mouth has around 10,000 taste buds, each of them able to detect only one of the four tastes. The mouth can detect only those substances which are presented directly to it, or are dissolved in and modified by saliva. The nose, on the other hand, gets its data from airborne molecules which either enter via the nostrils on inhaled air, or are carried from the mouth via the back of the throat into the nasal cavity. The epithelial cells in the nose are programmed to respond to a vast variety of odours. The air, having entered the nostrils or come up the throat, passes over three bony surfaces known as the turbinate bones on its way to the olfactory receptors. The latter consist of two small patches, one at the top of either nasal septum. Each of those patches contains about 10 million receptor cells. As if that were not enough, the lining of the turbinate bones serves to increase the effective area of the epithelium (the active surface) and some recent studies have suggested that there are glands in the nose which discharge proteins which, binding with aroma components, increase the concentration of the latter in the nasal mucus by a factor of 1000 to 10000 times. Even at the lower of these two figures, that makes the nose some two million times as sensitive as the mouth.

The olfactory epithelium (the surface on which smells are detected) is host to these millions of receptor neurons, each of which is a bit like a bulb in the soil: the receptor neuron is the bulb, from which neural tissue reaches up to the surface of the epithelium and down to the olfactory nerve. At the upper end, the neuron terminates in a number of hair-like cilia which are embedded in a layer of mucus. At the lower end, the olfactory nerve makes its way to the olfactory bulb at the base of the skull. About a thousand different proteins are bound to the surface of the olfactory membrane. When an odour molecule comes along, it attaches to one of these proteins, causing the neuron to fire an electrical signal. That signal makes its way via the olfactory bulb to the brain and we register the conscious experience of a particular smell. Olfactory receptors are the only neurons which have a connection directly into the brain, which may explain something about the peculiar immediacy and emotional power of smells.

While a certain amount is understood about the process of binding to odour molecules which causes the olfactory neuron to fire, there is as yet no generally accepted theory of smell which relates chemical structure to subjective experience. A few main trends have been identified, but nothing which could stand as a general theory of smell. So in any account of our perception of aromas, we can put scent names to a number of compounds, but we cannot say in advance how we will experience any novel compound. Both composition and structure of the odorant molecule seem to make a difference. Different isomers of the same molecule smell different. (If you have two molecules with the same makeup but the one is the mirror image of the other, they are called isomers.) For example, one isomer of carvone smells of caraway while its opposite image smells of spearmint.

Despite all this fancy equipment, humans are pretty low in the smelling stakes. Dogs are about 100 times more sensitive than we are. We think about where we are in the world in terms of a picture of our surroundings – a map – which is a visual image or representation. Dogs on the other hand, appear to have an olfactory geography. That is, they use scent to know where they are: both their own scent and that of other dogs as well as miscellaneous scents which are not dog-generated. When your mutt pisses on a lamppost, he doesn't do it to relieve himself: he is marking his territory so that other dogs sniffing the lamppost will know it's his. It has been suggested that there was an evolutionary advantage to gregarious humans in not being able to smell their family and neighbours, which accounted for their smell thresholds declining from a previously high level. This doesn't seem too plausible: dogs are at least as gregarious as humans and presumably smell their fellows' feet as acutely. Dogs appear positively to enjoy the smell of other dogs' urine and various things besides which it's probably unnecessary to mention.

People vary greatly in their sensitivity to smells, as they do to tastes. Some poor souls suffer from a condition known as anosmia, and are unable to detect all but the grossest of odours and those only at high concentrations. Selective odour-blindness is fairly common, though: some 47% of people are thought to suffer from insensitivity to the smell of urine and around 3% to the smell of sweaty feet. Anosmic people are mostly in the happy position of not knowing what they are missing, like the colour-blind, and the fact that some of them can get away with presenting themselves as connoisseurs, says more about the class of connoisseurs and it milieu than it does about the realities of the perception of aroma.

There is a rare condition known as hyperosmia, in which humans can become extremely sensitive to smell. Oliver Sachs describes a man who, for a period of a few weeks, suddenly and unexpectedly became able to detect very low levels of odour. During that period, he could identify other people by their smell, as a dog would do. This suggests that our inability to discern very low levels of odours is due to something more than the mere absence of adequate olfactory equipment.

We smell some compounds much more easily than we do others. Obviously, some things don't have a smell as far as humans are concerned, while other things are very smelly indeed. Top of the list is a group of substances known variously as thiols or mercaptans. These are organo-sulphur compounds which are best known to us as the smells of skunk and foxes. The fox uses its scent as a marker, whereas the skunk uses its as a weapon. The thiol emitted by skunk is so powerful that it can be detected at a great distance – it is not uncommon to smell it while driving on the freeway in some parts of the USA. It's about as nasty as smells get and I am told that if you are unfortunate enough to be sprayed by a skunk, it is a most traumatic experience, the memory of which lingers long.

The mode of our detection of odours varies greatly. Some odours are experienced as increasingly intense as the concentration of the odorant increases. With others odours, however, this is not the case: as soon as we smell the odour, it seems quite intense and the intensity does not appear to increase thereafter, even though there is a lot more of the substance present. This happens with vanilla and with some sulphur compounds. Some wine odours are very delicate and difficult to detect while others, such as the trichloroanisoles which produce corkiness (see the chapter Bad Tastes, page 155), are discernible at very low thresholds.

Smell, like taste, is affected by external conditions. Women are better at smelling than men – though women's abilities are affected by the hormonal changes caused by their menstrual cycle. The young smell more acutely than the old – though they may be less able to identify odours, mainly through inexperience. We learn what scents to look for and how to look for them and such learned abilities will tend to make up for any loss of sensitivity, at least until, in our seventies or eighties, the rate of replacement of olfactory neurons declines. We have difficulty in smelling when we have an infection of the nasal sinus or upper respiratory tract, mainly because the mucus produced in response to the infection blocks the air passages and prevents the transport of odour molecules to the olfactory epithelium. Smoking has an adverse effect on our ability to perceive odours, though for the most part the damage is reversible if you stop smoking for long enough. Obviously, someone else's smoke affects how a non-smoker will perceive any odours in the immediate vicinity.

We can often smell each of two different odours when they are perceived together, though we are unable to detect them when either is present on its own. This is obviously important in the flavour of wine, where all of the aroma constituents occur and are perceived together, as a single experience. The separation of aromas, which we do when we try to describe the flavour of a wine, is rather an artificial sort of thing. This is probably why the vocabulary of wine flavour is so poor.

Our sense of smell, like our sense of taste, is affected by what went before, for some smells mask and other smells enhance each other. We become habituated to smells as we do to other bodily sensations and if a smell is constantly present, we soon cease to register it. This is both a nuisance and a convenience in tasting wine. The tendency to blank out smells means that when you are tasting a wine, you have only a brief period in which to identify aromas before they disappear. We shall come to this later, in the section on practical tasting: there are simple ways to overcome the problem. It is a convenience because our diminishing sensitivity to one odour can allow other, weaker scents to become perceptible.

WINE FLAVOURS

DESCRIBING FLAVOUR

All sciences start with naming things: you classify different sorts of things by giving them names and the names serve as useful labels when you want to refer to them. The 19th century was the high point of taxonomy, as this process is called. People collected specimens of just about every sort of object and gave them names. It was a harmless and mostly enjoyable activity which allowed scientific gentlemen (they were mostly but not invariably men) to indulge themselves in their favourite pursuits, to which they could give a gloss of high scientific seriousness without having to think too hard. Our museums are full of the results: case after case of butterflies, moths, flint arrowheads, kidney stones, fossils and the like. Each different kind of object is given a name, with the added attraction that the chap who names it gets to have his name as part of the scientific classification and so, in his own eyes at least, joins the immortals.

The naming process extends to any activity which requires us to make distinctions. When we learn to do something, we commonly speak about 'getting to know the ropes'. This is a metaphor drawn from sailing ships, whose technology was so much a part of the ordinary experience of English-speaking peoples that the phrase entered the language. A big sailing ship had literally hundreds of ropes: each had a unique function, and each had a unique name by which it could be identified. The first thing a newcomer to the ship had to do was to learn the names of the ropes. Until he could make this fundamental distinction, he was unable to take part in the working of the ship.

There are probably good gardeners who do not know the names of the plants in their garden. Certainly, knowing the scientific names is not necessary. But the making of the distinctions which names imply is absolutely essential. And whenever the solitary gardener requires to order seeds, or needs information – i.e. whenever he requires to speak to other people about his garden – he needs to have names for his plants.

It is a very curious thing that, though people have been making and drinking wines for thousands of years – and presumably talking to each other about the wines they made and drank – no specialised vocabulary of wine aromas has arisen in the ordinary language of any wine-producing or consuming country. Wine tasters have their own language which they use to describe wine odours but, like ordinary language, it contains few or no unique odour terms. Emile Peynaud, in his book *Le Gout du Vin*, lists over two hundred aroma terms which he has encountered in tasters' remarks and writings (see page 24). All are names or descriptions of the things smelled; none are terms which apply primarily to the odour.

The words we use to describe taste parallel the vocabulary of sight. 'Sweet', 'sour', 'salt' and 'bitter' are on a par with 'red', 'black', 'square' and 'round'. Each refers directly to a sensation. In describing smell we seem to lack direct referents of this sort and resort to naming the smell by reference, not to the sensation experienced, but to the object, or class of objects, smelled. Thus we say a wine smells of blackcurrants. We all know what blackcurrants are, and how they smell, but our language makes a distinction: we do not say that something smells blackcurrant, we say it smells *of* blackcurrant. It is a small difference, but significant. It is probably not significant of any great metaphysical division in the nature of experience, but of a variation which has its roots in the different neural pathways which nature has evolved for taste and smell.

Recent research has shown that, as children, we classify smells according to the event with which they are associated. Only later do we begin to arrange our olfactory experience by categories of similar odour. This may be related to the observation that newcomers to wine tasting often admit that they find it very difficult to identify any aromas at all. But with a list of possible odours before them, they discover an ability of which they were unaware. While an element of autosuggestion may be present, this effect is so striking that it suggests the initial problem is one of categorisation rather than perception and it lends credence to the notion that the difference lies in the brain.

WINE FLAVOURS

The classification of tastes – as distinct from flavours – is straightforward. We experience four sorts of taste in the mouth and we give a name to each, just as we give different names to differently coloured butterflies – but with tastes it's simpler, there being only four of them. Unhappily, as so often with the simple things in life, uncertainty lurks just around the corner. There exists at least one other taste, of which people in the Western world were unaware until recently: so unaware, indeed, that there is no word for it in English. Yet millions of people have known of it for a very long time, for it occurs naturally in the decomposition of the proteins in meat. In Japanese, it is called *umami*, the name by which we now know it: it is the flavour of monosodium glutamate and the mouth appears to be equipped with specialised receptors for detecting it. Most Western consumers will be aware of it only as a component of Chinese food: not as a definite flavour, but as an enhancement of other flavours. It has been used in China and Japan for centuries and is now widely used in the processed-food industry, where it is so powerful a component of flavour that its presence makes palatable foodstuffs which otherwise would be insipid. As far as is known, it has not been used in wine. (Meaty aromas are not uncommon in wines. Whether there is any relationship with umami is not known.) If it does nothing more, so recent a discovery of so basic a taste should make us cautious in our classification of flavours.

We have seen that the aroma is by far the greater part of the flavour of a wine. The identification of aromas is the business of so-called organoleptic analysis, a discipline which in the last two centuries has demonstrated (some) wines to have a surprising variety of flavours. Some flavours are pleasant to almost all people, some not. In between, there are flavours which are valued in some cultures and not in others. And there are flavours which may be pleasing when only faintly discerned, but disgusting when strong. Those flavours will figure largely in our discussion of wines, for they form the basis of much that distinguishes a fine wine from a merely good one.

Professionals usually distinguish between aroma and bouquet. The usage is variable, but generally as follows. 'Aroma' is the term given to the odour components which arise from the grapes used, while 'bouquet' describes odours which are created in the wine-making process and in the bottle. Aroma arises from the contents of the grape and from what happens to it while it is still on the vine (growth, ripening, over-ripening, disease, etc.). Bouquet is the product of everything which happens afterwards, from pressing through to maturation. There are three main categories of bouquet: fermentative bouquet, processing bouquet and ageing bouquet. Fermentative bouquet develops during each of the three main types of fermentation: yeast (alcoholic) fermentation, bacterial (malolactic) fermentation and grape-cell (carbonic) fermentation. Processing bouquets are found mainly in wines which have been subject to a greater degree of processing than ordinary wines: fractional blending, as in sherry; adding brandy, as in port; baking, as in madeira, and yeast autolysis, which is what gives sparkling wines their sparkle. Ageing bouquet is acquired by the wine in cask after fermentation has ceased and in bottle after the wine has been bottled. In what follows, 'aroma' and 'bouquet' will be used interchangeably, except where the context requires a distinction to be made.

There is a fair amount of agreement as to the main classes of wine aroma, though tasters often differ as to specifics. The analysis of wine flavour is necessary whenever anyone wishes to describe a wine, or to differentiate one wine from another. Whenever wine moves out of the vineyard and into the marketplace, a vocabulary is required, for every seller needs to be able to describe his or her wares. Greek traders selling wine to the Romans and the Gauls reputedly employed over one hundred terms for describing their wines.

Detailed description of the flavours of wines in modern times began in the early 18th century, as a result of the demand created by English merchants for French wines. Fine wines fetched a premium price and, where a sale was proposed without tasting the product, a vocabulary was required to justify the differential. By the end of the 18th century, at least forty terms were being used to describe the flavours and other attributes of wines. The versatile Jean Antoine Chaptal greatly extended and systematised the taster's vocabulary in his *L'Art de Faire le Vin* of 1807. In the course of the 19th century, the (French) wine-tasting vocabulary had increased to about two hundred terms and today it numbers nearly five times that many.

The taxonomy of flavour in English was a much later development. In the late 1950s, Michael Broadbent wrote what was probably the first systematic work in English on the flavours of wines. It was a pamphlet designed for the use of professionals at Harveys of Bristol, but it soon found a wider readership. It was produced as a book in 1968 under the title of *Wine Tasting/Enjoying/Understanding*. The work was very influential, especially in the wine trade, and was reproduced in several European wine journals.

Around the same time, at the Bordeaux Institute of Oenology,

Professor Peynaud and his colleagues were elaborating a vocabulary
for the description of wines, and seeking to link the flavour
description to what was known scientifically about the components
of wines. This work found expression in *Le Gout du Vin*, by Emile
Peynaud, which was first published in 1980. This is an extraordinary
work: discursive and opinionated, analytic and speculative, scientific
and artistic, it is very French. It also makes considerable demands of
the reader, which may be why it is so hard to find a copy in English,
despite its having been ably translated by Michael Schuster, who
himself is the author of a number of distinguished books on wine.

Peynaud lists over two hundred wine odours which have been
encountered in tasters' writings. He divides them into ten classes.
Here is his complete list.

Animal
Amber, game, game stew, venison stew, fur, wet dog, musk, musky,
civet, sweat, wool fat, mouse urine, cat urine, meaty, indole, skatole,
gamey, fresh sea fish.

Balsamic
Cade oil, juniper, pine, pitch pine, resin, resinous, turpentine,
incense, vanilla.

Woody
Green wood, old wood, rancio wood, acacia, oak, cedar, sandalwood,
lead pencil, cigar box, barrel stave, bark, woody.

Chemical
Acetic, alcohol, carbonic, hydrocarbons, napthol, phenol, carbolic,
sulphured, sulphurated, sulphurised, sulphurous, celluloid, ebonite,
medicinal, pharmaceutical, disinfectant, iodine, chlorine, graphite.

Spicy
Aniseed, dill, Chinese anise, fennel, mushroom, agaric, chanterelle
mushroom, boletus mushroom, truffle, cinnamon, ginger, clove, nutmeg,
pepper, green pepper, basil, spearmint, thyme, angelica, liquorice, garlic,
onion, oregano, marjoram, lavender, camphor, vermouth.

Empyreumatic
Smoke, tobacco, incense, burnt, grilled, caramel, grilled almonds,
toast, rubbed flints, gunflint, silex, gunpowder, burnt wood, fire,
rubber, leather, Russian leather, roasted coffee, cocoa, chocolate.

Estery
Isoamyl acetate, acetone, amyl alcohol, banana, acid drops, pear

drops, nail varnish, higher fatty acid esters (caprates, caproates, caprylates), soap, candle, candle wax, stearin, yeast, ferments, dough, wheat, beer, cider, lactic, sour milk, milk products, cheese, butter, diacetyl, yoghurt, sauerkraut, sackcloth, cow shed, stable.

Floral
Fowery, floral, the blossom of acacia, almond, orange, apple, pear, elder, grapevine, hawthorn, sweet briar, honeysuckle, lemon, hyacinth, narcissus, jasmine, geranium, pelargonium, heather, broom, marsh mallow, magnolia, honey, peony, mignonette, rose, camomile, lime, verbena, iris, violet, clove, carnation.

Fruity
Raisins, crystallised fruit, grapes, raisiny, muscat-like, black cherry, morello cherry, whiteheart cherry, kirsch, cherry brandy, plum, prune, sloe, mirabelle, fruit stones, bitter almond, pistachio, wild berries, small red fruits, bilberry, blackcurrant, strawberry, wild strawberry, raspberry, redcurrant, mulberry, apricot, quince, peach, pear, apple, melon, citrus fruits, bergamot, lemon, lime, orange, grapefruit, pineapple, banana, dried fig, fig-like, pomegranate, walnut, hazelnut, green olive, black olive.

Vegetal
Grass, herbaceous, pasture, hay, meadow smells, green leaves, bindweed, rubbed blackcurrant leaf, drying vegetation, dried leaves, bay leaf, herb tea, dead leaves, artemisia, cabbage, cress, ivy, garden mercury, French marigold, horseradish, radish, French fern, green coffee beans, tea, tobacco, leaf mould, dust, undergrowth, earth, earthy, march, tree moss.

It should be noted that Peynaud does not present these flavours as a definitive or an exhaustive list. He merely reports that at one time or another, he has seen or heard them used to describe wine. But he does give them his imprimatur, saying that all these smells really can be found in wine. He complements the list by an extensive discussion of the vocabularies of balance, structure, alcoholic strength, acidity, sweetness, bitterness and carbon dioxide. He also discusses the use of metaphors to describe wines. We are concerned mainly with the flavours of wines, but it may not be amiss to look briefly at those other aspects of the pleasure which people derive from them.

Balance is something we seek in wine. All wines, even the most basic, possess a number of flavours, so when we taste a wine, our perception of any given flavour is modified by the presence of other flavours. This is also true of almost all foodstuffs. An egg without salt tastes very different from an egg with salt. It is the combination of the flavours of the egg and the salt which we find pleasing. Neither egg nor salt on its own tastes nice and there is a gradation of flavour from all egg and no salt, which is nasty, through to all salt and no egg, which is also nasty. In the middle we have egg with salt, which is nice. So with wines: balance is everything. At its simplest, a white wine which is very acid is rendered palatable by having high levels of sugar. Without the sugar it would be undrinkable. But without the acidity, that amount of sweetness would be unpalatable. Alcohol, too, balances acidity: not only because alcohol is sweet-tasting, but because the sensation it causes somehow moderates our perception of the acidity. Also, white wines which are intensely aromatic will tolerate much higher acidity than those which are not.

Balance in red wines is rather more complicated, not least because red wines have a more complex make-up than whites, at least as regards their principal flavour components. Red wines are usually less acidic than whites, but contain much higher levels of phenolic compounds. If acidity is combined with a lot of tannins, the resultant wine will be harsh and astringent. On the other hand, if the acidity is less but the alcohol level high, a very high level of tannins will be acceptable. Happily, both tannins and acidity tend to decline as a wine matures, hence the ability of wines which are harsh when young to become well-balanced and delicious after some years in bottle. Other flavour components, especially the volatile ones, also play a large part in the balance of a wine, though, because they are so difficult to identify, one suspects that the attribution of pleasing flavour to balance partakes of a fair amount of post hoc reasoning.

Structure is a quality commonly attributed to wines. In my experience, most people who talk about the structure of a wine don't have the faintest idea of what it means, and I recommend as a source of harmless fun the practice of asking anyone who uses structural terms just exactly what he or she means by them. If you can get past the condescension which for some reason often accompanies the discovery of structural qualities in a wine, you may or may not hear something which makes sense. Peynaud describes structure as being a visual image which always accompanies the sensation of taste. He says that when we have various flavour sensations simultaneously (don't we always?), we experience a taste profile which causes the wine to convey an idea of thickness, or of structure in three dimensions. This semi-solid, three-dimensional impression changes progressively as we hold the wine in the mouth and eventually swallow. It is this which gives rise to descriptions of the wine as being long or short, formless or round, flat or angular. While no doubt the vocabulary is useful to those who are familiar with it, it is open to accusations of obscurantism and one suspects that the same information might be conveyed more plausibly and accurately by systematising the description of mouth-feel. The idea of a visual image of flavour is a good one, though, which we shall come to shortly.

In the early 1980s, Ann Noble and her colleagues at the University of California at Davis developed a comprehensive vocabulary of descriptive wine flavour terms. These they presented in the form of the Aroma Wheel. The terms are more comprehensible to persons of an English-speaking background – and especially an American-English – than are Peynaud's. They are also much more rigorously analytic than Peynaud's, consisting purely of descriptive terms and omitting completely value-judgements as well as vague and metaphorical descriptions. For those reasons, they have been adopted as the basis of the flavour discussion in this book. Peynaud's work is extraordinary, informative and highly entertaining, but it is very discursive and prolix. And, there are more than enough obscurities in the language of wine without avoidable obfuscation.

THE AROMA WHEEL

The Aroma Wheel will be familiar to most students of wine flavour. Flavours are arranged in three tiers of generality. At the highest level are the 12 main classes of odour. These are divided into 29 subclasses, and the latter into a total of 94 recognisable odours.
The Aroma Wheel is pictured on pages 32–33. Set out in tabular form, its divisions are as follows:

Tier 1	Tier 2	Tier 3
Floral	Floral	Linalool
		Orange blossom
		Rose
		Violet
		Geranium
Spicy	Spicy	Cloves
		Black pepper
		Liquorice, anise

Fruity	Citrus	Grapefruit
		Lemon
	Berry	Blackberry
		Raspberry
		Strawberry
		Blackcurrant
	Tree fruit	Cherry
		Apricot
		Peach
		Apple
	Tropical fruit	Pineapple
		Melon
		Banana
	Dried fruit	Strawberry jam
		Raisin
		Prune
		Fig
	Other fruit	Artificial fruit
		Methyl anthranilate
Vegetative	Fresh	Stemmy
		Grass (cut, green)
		Bell pepper
		Eucalyptus
		Mint
	Canned cooked	Green beans
		Asparagus
		Green olive
		Black olive
		Artichoke
	Dried	Haystraw
		Tea
		Tobacco
Nutty	Nutty	Walnut
		Hazelnut
		Almond
Caramelised	Caramelised	Honey
		Butterscotch
		Diacetyl (butter)

		Soy sauce
		Chocolate
		Molasses
Woody	Phenolic	Phenolic
		Vanilla
	Resinous	Cedar
		Oak
	Burned	Smoky
		Burnt toast
		Coffee
Earthy	Mouldy	Dusty
		Mushroom
	Earthy	Musty (mildew)
		Mouldy cork
Chemical	Petroleum	Tar
		Plastic
		Kerosene
		Diesel
	Sulphur	Rubbery
		Hydrogen sulphide
		Mercaptan
		Garlic
		Skunk
		Cooked cabbage
		Burnt match
		Sulphur dioxide
		Wet wool, wet dog
	Papery	Filter pad
		Wet cardboard
	Pungent	Ethyl acetate
		Acetic acid
		Ethanol
		Sulphur dioxide
	Other	Fishy
		Soapy
		Sorbate
		Fusel alcohol
Pungent	Hot	Alcohol
	Cool	Menthol

Oxidised	Oxidised	Acetaldehyde
Microbiological	Yeasty	Flor yeast
		Leesy
	Lactic	Sauerkraut
		Butyric acid
		Sweaty
		Lactic acid
	Other	Horsey
		Mousey

Because the perception of odour is to some extent subjective, everyone finds things in the wheel with which he or she disagrees, but as an analytic tool, it is immensely valuable. Note that its terms are purely descriptive: it does not include hedonic or evaluative terms such as 'smooth' or 'supple'.

Since Peynaud and Noble are both respected professionals in the field, we would expect there to be a fair degree of correspondence between the two aroma lists. Three of Peynaud's categories correspond closely to those of the Aroma Wheel: Floral, Fruity and Spicy. Almost all of the third-tier flavours in those sections of the Aroma Wheel are to be found in the corresponding Peynaud class. A further three classes correspond in title with the Aroma Wheel. They are Vegetal, Woody and Chemical, although the correspondence of the actual aromas is poor. Of the 16 aromas in the vegetative group of the Aroma Wheel, only 6 are to be found in Peynaud's list and only 3 of those in his Vegetal class. All 6 aromas listed by the Wheel as being Woody are in Peynaud's list, but only 2, Cedar and Oak, are in his Woody section. Of 23 aromas listed by the Wheel as being of a Chemical nature, only 8 are anywhere in Peynaud's list and 3 of those listed by him as being Chemical. Peynaud does not use separate classifications for Nutty, Caramelised, Earthy, Pungent, Oxidised and Microbiological aromas. He does on the other hand list aromas as being Animal, Balsamic, Empyreumatic and Estery.

The difference between the two systems is probably less than it appears. Peynaud is reporting terms which people have used, without comment, save for saying that all the flavours listed can be found in some wine. We may presume that all the terms were used by professional wine tasters for a mainly European audience and a good many of them for fellow-professionals. That is some way from the Aroma Wheel, whose (very successful) purpose it was to act as a teaching aid for students of oenology, and to popularise the analytical tasting of wines. This, and the restrictions of space imposed by the wheel device, explains why Peynaud's list has so many more flavours than does the Aroma Wheel.

And we might mention the large cultural difference: the principal readership for the Wine Aroma Wheel in its present manifestation is North American: the olfactory experience of US citizens is significantly different from that of most Europeans – and I'm not referring only to the inclusion of Skunk (a very distinctive odour; a useful part of one's aroma lexicon, but not an experience one would seek to repeat). Most people in the USA in the course of their daily lives are exposed to a much smaller range of smells than their counterparts in Europe, and especially in France.

The terms in the Aroma Wheel may be divided roughly into those which describe desirable flavours and those used to refer to off-odours. From Floral down to Caramelised, the categories include those odours whose presence is looked on with favour by most wine drinkers. Woody flavours may or may not be approved: Vanilla is usually agreeable; Burnt Toast less so. From Earthy onward the flavours are to be avoided, though even here there are exceptions. Many of the off-odours may contribute to the bouquet of a wine if present at very low concentrations. It is not unusual to find sulphurous aromas in very old wines: their presence at very low levels contributes to the overall bouquet of the wine. Our perception thresholds for such compounds are very low, however, and the presence of anything more than a trace will render the wine quite foul. Other off-odours may be acceptable in one wine but not in another. Most wines which are heavily oxidised are considered undrinkable, but sherry makers go to great lengths to ensure that their wines are oxidised. The acetaldehyde aroma of sherry is something of an acquired taste – but there are many sherry drinkers who do not regret the acquisition.

The list of aromas includes one major category which refers to mouth-feel rather than aroma. I refer, of course, to the primary category of Pungent. This, which is subdivided into hot and cool, exemplified by Alcohol and Menthol respectively, is not the result of stimulation of the nerves of the olfactory epithelium. It functions by means of the trigeminal nerve and refers to sensations which are different from those of taste or smell, though obviously congruent to them. Its inclusion in the Aroma Wheel is quite justifiable, however, given the main purpose of the Wheel, which is to impart information about sensation to would-be wine tasters.

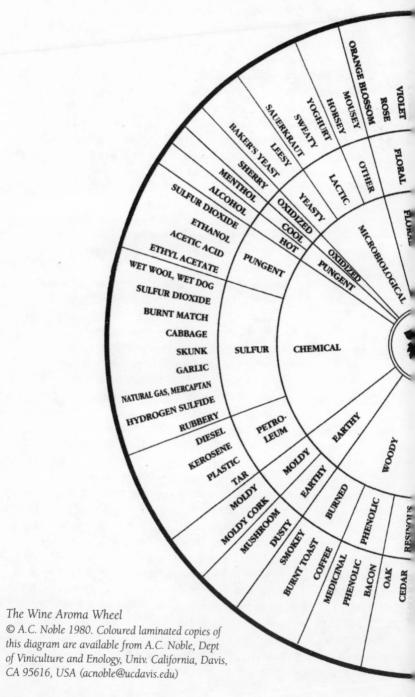

The Wine Aroma Wheel
© A.C. Noble 1980. Coloured laminated copies of
this diagram are available from A.C. Noble, Dept
of Viniculture and Enology, Univ. California, Davis,
CA 95616, USA (acnoble@ucdavis.edu)

Fruity flavours are the most numerous of the pleasant aromas. Blackcurrant is the most familiar, being characteristic of red wines made from common grape varietals such as Cabernet Sauvignon, Merlot and Shiraz. Others of the berry fruits are to be found in red wines, while citrus and tropical-fruit flavours more commonly occur in whites. The presence of fruity odours may be caused by esters which form when an alcohol reacts with an acid, though there are lots of other components and the make-up of fruit aromas can be complex and varied.

The possible range of floral aromas is huge and the Aroma Wheel's restriction of the number of florals to five probably owes more to lack of space than it does to the possibilities of wine aromas. Commonly remarked aromas in addition to those mentioned include lily, iris, gardenia, hyacinth, jasmine, magnolia and carnation. However, not all wine tasters are also gardeners, so it isn't too surprising if they don't recognise some of the more esoteric blooms. While floral flavours are present to some degree in the aroma of most good wines, they are at their most striking in wines made from grapes such as Riesling and Gewürztraminer.

Fruity and floral aromas are part of everyone's experience, and therefore easy to describe. Vegetal odours are less easy to identify. The group of odours which comprises the scent of new-mown hay, of green beans, of green peppers and of beetroots is not one most folk would actually seek and remember. Many of those odours, indeed, are far from pleasant in other than trace amounts. With a little practice, however, it is possible to identify such odours at quite low concentrations, and it is apparent that their presence at low levels contributes to the flavour of many wines. Vegetative aromas derive most commonly from Sauvignon blanc grapes: think of the flavour of a good Sancerre and it will be obvious that vegetative aroma can be a constituent of really fine wine. While in our experience vegetative flavours seem very different from fruity or flowery odours, they can be quite close chemically. The fresh smell of newly picked raspberries is partly due to the presence of ionone, an organic compound which also gives us the aroma of dried hay and violets.

The range of spicy aromas in the Aroma Wheel is surprisingly small. In circumstances where we encounter those which are mentioned, we generally also find nutmeg and mace, cinnamon and fenugreek, as well as other, less well-known spices. However, the term 'spice' in ordinary English usage covers a very wide range of flavourings and its reference has more to do with the historical origins of the flavours than it does with any organoleptic congruence.

This is more evident in omissions than in inclusion: neither mustard nor horseradish is classed as a spicy flavour, though both are fierce enough to make us weep and horseradish is included in Peynaud's list as a Vegetal aroma. That they are rarely classed with the oriental spices is probably because they are indigenous to northern Europe and therefore have not been regarded as exotic by English-speaking peoples. Asafoetida, on the other hand, is so classed, though in its flavour it has nothing in common with cloves or pepper. This is explained by its being widely used in Indian cooking. Its flavour would certainly be among the sulphurous, Chemical odours of the Aroma Wheel, alongside skunk and garlic. It provides perhaps the best example of a flavour which, present at low levels, is highly desirable, but which beyond a low threshold is perfectly foul. There is a flavour found in white Burgundies, referred to as 'gunflint' or 'flinty', which would better be described as that of asafoetida. The flinty flavour is sometimes mistakenly thought to be something to do with the dryness of pebbles, but in fact it refers to the sulphurous odour which is released when the flint of a flintlock gun is snapped. So few people nowadays have any experience of firing a flintlock that the term has come to be misunderstood.

Nutty flavours are to be found in many wines at low levels, but particularly in fino and amontillado sherries, where they are by-products of the flor yeast which is encouraged to grow on top of the sherry. The yeast also produces acetaldehyde (see page 71), which gives sherries their characteristic oxidised flavour. Acetaldehyde itself has a nutty aroma.

The group of flavours we class as caramel-related is one we associate with sweet things, probably because almost all of us have eaten toffee, at least as children, and most toffee brings together the flavours of sugar, butter and vanilla. Caramel proper is produced when sugar is heated. The sugar molecules break down and coagulate to make sticky or solid caramel, depending on how much heat is applied and for how long. Every toffee-maker knows how you test the progress of the toffee by letting the molten sugar cool as it slides over the back of a spoon, or by dropping it into cold water. Some of the sugars break up and their incorporation into the caramel gives it its flavour. The flavour component of caramel is an aldehyde, not so very different from the acetaldehyde mentioned above, and composed of the same atoms (though in a different arrangement) as the vanilla in the next flavour category.

Butter owes much of its flavour to diacetyl, which is made of the same stuff. It, too, is pleasing in small doses but not in large. It is the principal component of the smell of old sweat. New sweat is odourless, but the skin bacteria which feed on it produce diacetyl, which is quite smelly. Remember what we said above, about how you can identify an odour much more easily if you have the idea of it in mind. Sniff your armpits after a long, hot day if you would become familiar with diacetyl. Then take a glass of wine and think 'armpit' as you sniff it.

With woody flavours, there is great variation in the levels of tolerable flavour. The presence of vanilla is almost always desirable, and vanilla, as we have mentioned before, is a flavour which is peculiarly incapable of overstatement. Some of the greatest red wines in the world have a vanilla flavour. Oakiness, however, is another matter. There can be few drinkers who are unfamiliar with the practice of some Australian wine makers of producing white wines, mostly Chardonnays, which are very heavily oaked. I can't say I care for the stuff myself, but there can be no doubt that a lot of people do, for it finds a very large market. The same goes for the resinous wines produced in Greece and Cyprus.

The earthy aromas mark the divide between nice and nasty flavours. Though some of them are fine in small quantities – a bit of mushroom can be pleasant – others, such as mustiness and mouldy cork, are well into the realms of the horrible. Corkiness especially can be detected at very low levels. There are several possible causes of corky odours, involving bacteria or fungi or both, and they may come from either cork or cooperage. The most common, however, is chlorine compound 2.4.6-trichloroanisole, which is the result of a fungus which feeds on cork that has been treated with – ironically – a common fungicide, pentachlorophenol. It can also arise if chlorine has been used to bleach the cut cork. However it comes, you are in no doubt about it when the bottle is opened. (See pages 155–163 on bad tastes.)

The class of chemical off-odours is much the largest. It contains, especially among the sulphur compounds, some of the foulest off-notes which can be found in a wine. But even here we find odours which, though normally disgusting, may contribute to the bouquet of a fine wine if present as only the faintest background odour. We mentioned asafoetida, above, as being to Indian cuisine what a whiff of sulphur can be to a great white Burgundy. That, however, is about all you can say for this class of odours. They are almost invariably disgusting, and in lots of different ways which only the gustatory masochist would care to explore. (That said, you can acquire a taste for some. I'm very fond of big old diesel engines, and find the smell of diesel not unpleasant.)

Pungency, we have already covered. It is a mouth-feel, rather than a flavour. Alcohol feels hot because it stimulates pain nerve-endings and menthol creates an impression of coolness by causing the coolness sensors to become active at a much higher temperature than usual.

Oxidised flavours are caused by the presence of acetaldehyde (see above). This may arise from exposure of wine to the air, in which case it is undesirable. If it is cultivated, as it is in sherry, it can be a component of a pleasant flavour.

The microbiological odours have coherence, at least – they all smell more or less like each other. This is because they arise from a group of related compounds, which are created by the action of microorganisms. None of them are pleasant, even when barely perceptible.

DESCRIBING FLAVOUR

A perusal of any of the many wine guides – those which tell you about individual wines: what they taste like and what they cost – provides an interesting perspective on the use of flavour terminology. Few of them make much pretence of objective assessment of the wines in terms of their flavour. The typical entry is made up of four or five components. First, there are tasting notes, the part which tries to tell you something of how the wine tastes. These consist of two sorts of terms: descriptive and hedonic. The descriptive terms refer to the types of flavour and its strength; the hedonic are judgemental, and tell you how the taster feels about the wine. The two are usually well mixed up, and if it is well done, you come away with an idea of whether the taster liked the flavour and what were the principal tastes and aromas. Then the price is usually given, and sometimes there is a further level of judgement, as to whether this is good value for money or not. Some writers use a rating system, which indicates the quality of the wine, irrespective of price.

With reputable wine critics, one can generally rely on the veracity of the judgement: even if the writer has been unduly influenced as regards certain wines, only a few of the many descriptions are likely to be tainted. And the writer's preferences are usually so well known that one can make allowances for inevitable bias. Indeed, writers like Oz Clarke and Malcolm Gluck make no secret about their preferences, so we can easily adjust their ratings to our own likes and dislikes. We cannot, alas, say as much for the descriptions which appear on the labels of supermarket wines. It is rare nowadays to find a wine on a supermarket shelf which does not bear tasting notes which purport to describe the wine. There are very strict rules as to what the label must say about how much the bottle contains, the percentage of pure alcohol, and the place where the wine is made; the vineyard or château name is a legally guarded trademark; but there are no rules which say the tasting notes must tell the truth. There are lies, damned lies and tasting notes on the backs of bottles, and of the three, the last is the worst. We can – or some people can – always say snobbishly that the bottles we get from our wine merchant don't do anything so vulgar. But this won't do: the supermarkets have brought wine to the great mass of the people in countries which do not make their own wines, and to most of those in countries which do. Like it or not, that is how much of the world's wine production is going to be sold in the 21st century, so there ought to be some regulation of tasting notes.

The problem is, how? As we have seen, taste is notoriously subjective. And even supposing standards could be established, to regulate the flavour information for all bottlings of all wines would require a gustatory bureaucracy whose expense would add substantially to the cost of our wine. But some standardisation of the supply of information does seem possible. If there were such a thing, it could form the basis of the contract between buyer and seller, which would be actionable at law. The mere possibility of such an action would constrain wine makers to provide reasonably accurate information.

So how do we provide that information? Chemical analysis is a well-established scientific technique and one which is widely used in the wine industry. Analysis can identify many of the flavour components of wines, but, alas, there is not sufficient congruence between analytic and organoleptic categories (a fancy way of saying that the scientists can't put names to the things which give us all the flavours in a wine) for this to work in practice. And there is the problem of presentation: a tasting panel can say pretty accurately how a wine tastes, but how do we show the result?

FLAVOUR PROFILES

The Aroma Wheel is a useful graphic device, but it is difficult to read and the placing of categories alongside each other has led a number of people, in the wine industry and elsewhere, to assume a congruence between adjacent odours which in many cases plainly does not exist. Various attempts have been made to present flavour in the form of a graphic based on the Aroma Wheel. The trouble with this device is that it is also difficult to read. It requires to be rotated to be read, which is a nuisance, and it is counter-intuitive, by which I mean that you have to make a considerable effort to extract any sense out of it every time you read it. It doesn't get much easier with practice, either. (These are not faults of the Aroma Wheel, which is an economical and useful device for its intended purpose: the exhibition of flavour information at three levels of generality.)

There follows a suggestion for a flavour graphic which uses the categories of the Aroma Wheel, but provides flavour information in a more economical and understandable way.

In indicating the general character and quality of a wine, it is sufficient to class flavours according to the first-level categories of the Aroma Wheel, plus the three tongue tastes of sweet, sour and bitter. That gives us 15 criteria by means of which to judge a wine. It leaves out mouth-feel and hedonic judgement. The first is not necessary, given an accurate indication of flavour, and the second is subjective. If we were to have 15 reliable criteria we would be going a long way down the road to providing a trustworthy indicator for the great majority of wines. It wouldn't do for really great wines, but then really great wines probably aren't going to appear in the supermarket and don't need such a thing.

The Flavour Profile consists of a bar chart, whose vertical axis is numerical, on a scale of, say, one to ten, and whose horizontal axis is labelled with the flavour categories in the following order: Sweet, Sour, Bitter, Floral, Fruity, Vegetative, Caramelised, Spicy, Nutty, Oxidised, Earthy, Woody, Pungent, Chemical, and Microbiological.

The bars on the chart show the absolute level of the various flavours, and the position and relationship of the bars indicates the nature of the wine. For the Flavour Profile to be meaningful, it requires to be calibrated and for the calibration to be free of subjectivity. (Your ten score for sweetness might be my seven, for example.) It is probably impossible, given that taste is a subjective sensation, for this to be done precisely, but in practice it isn't too difficult to scale each of the flavour categories so that there will be a fair measure of agreement. By using standard wines, each of which exhibits the desired characteristic in very high degree, it should be possible to reach a consensus. So for sweetness we might choose one of the richest muscats, which would score ten, while a bone-dry red would score zero.

Since sweetness is the result of the sugar which remains in the wine after fermentation (or is added subsequently), known as residual sugar, it is possible to have a scientific measure of sweetness, simply by measuring the amount of sugar. This, however, would not serve our purpose, since what is wanted is an indication of the subjective impression of the sweetness of the wine, and this depends not only on the absolute sugar level, but on that level relative to certain other factors, principally acidity.

The order in which the flavours appear on the chart is arbitrary. The mouth flavours appear first, for those are always present in some degree. The ambiguous flavours appear after those which are more generally desirable, and the unequivocally unpleasant flavours at the end. Thus, a chart which has low bars in the first two-thirds and high bars at the end indicates a bad wine. To say what makes a good wine is more problematic, since quality in a wine requires not only the presence of desirable flavours, but a combination of certain of them. As we remarked in the first chapter, good wine is distinguished from other, lesser potations by the presence of a large number of flavours, all at low levels of intensity. So a good wine is likely to show a broad spread of flavours, none at too high a level.

Floral and fruity flavours obviously belong together, being chemically closely related. So, too, are the members of the caramel-spicy-nutty group – related, that is, though not necessarily chemically, since 'spicy' covers such a large field.

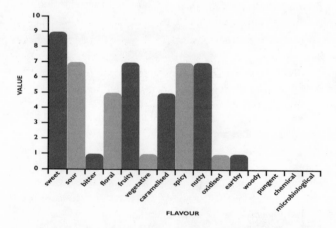

The wine profiled above is one made mainly from the muscat grape. It has a high alcohol content, which serves to enhance the already sweet taste. The sweetness, however, is balanced by a high acidity, which prevents the wine becoming flaccid and cloying. There is little bitterness, as one would expect of such a wine and it is high in floral and fruity flavours, and in the caramel-spicy-nutty group.

Altogether a highly flavoured wine: not one noted for its subtlety but popular as a dessert wine.

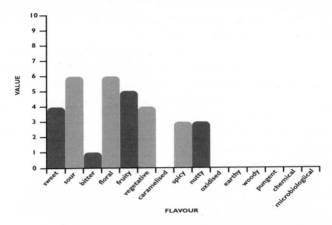

The Sancerre described above is a much superior wine, despite – or perhaps because of – much lower levels of flavour. This is a dry Loire wine whose acidity overpowers its sweetness to give an impression of sharpness. It is nonetheless high in fruit and floral aromas and has a background of spicy nuttiness, which, taken together, make it a very good wine indeed.

Here we have a young claret from the Bordeaux region. This is a good, young, red Bordeaux. Not a Grand Cru, but from a vineyard of some repute among those knowledgeable in such things. It is a wine which is good now and will probably get better over time, as the tannins decline from their present, not-very-high levels and the other flavours come more into balance. What is noticeable about it is the

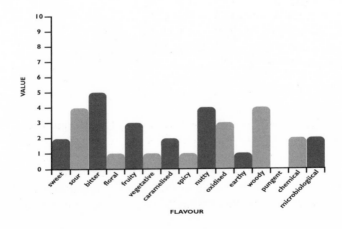

sheer spread of flavours: all the nice ones and some of the dodgy ones as well. The latter are expected to decline along with the tannins, though not ever to disappear, persisting as a background funkiness against which the other, higher aromas show themselves off at their best.

A fino sherry shows a quite different profile. Here the oxidised components create a peak against a background of generally pleasant flavours, of which the nutty group are the most prominent.

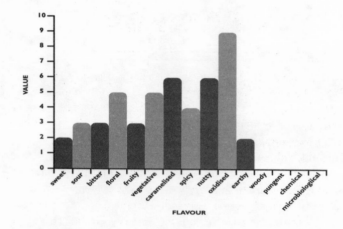

FLAVOUR ORIGINS
≈TASTE≈

We have already remarked that wine is pleasing to the taste because it contains all sorts of interesting compounds. This chapter is about some of those compounds – and, therefore, a lot of this chapter is about chemistry, for chemistry is the science of compounds. It is possible to appreciate wine without knowing much about its chemistry, but – following the principle that appreciation implies knowledge – it is desirable to know something.. It is a sad reflection on the way in which science is taught in schools that the mere mention of chemistry will be enough to cause many readers to skip this section. They assume that because their experiences of classroom chemistry were uniformly disagreeable, it is impossible for them to find any interest in the science thereafter. That is not the case, as I hope to demonstrate, so beg the reader to persevere.

The sciences – or at least the physical sciences, of which chemistry is one – make serious demands on our understanding. For those of us who are not professional scientists, the best we can expect is to comprehend some of the conclusions of scientific enquiry without necessarily grasping most of the theories which led to them. In some sciences even this is impossible, for the conclusions are so intimately bound up with the theory that the two cannot be separated. (Try reading some contemporary cosmology or quantum mechanics and you will get the idea.) Happily, that is not the case with the simpler bits of organic chemistry and biochemistry, which are the sciences necessary for an understanding of wine. Indeed the reverse is true: one can derive a lot of pleasure from treating chemistry as a spectator sport, enjoying the results without having to engage in the heavy thinking which produced them. That said, we should enter a caveat: don't expect too much from the chemistry of wine. Our concern is with the flavour of wines and, though our knowledge of what makes wines taste as they do has made great strides in the last century or so, we are still a long way from being able to produce a list of all the components of the flavour of a particular wine. This is because flavour depends as much on little things as it does on large. However, it helps to know about the large, and those we can describe in terms of simple chemistry. If the wine maker doesn't get the basics right, there is little point in our looking for finesse in the flavours of his or her wines: if the wine is too sweet or too bitter, the infinitesimal variations which provide the subtle flavours of a fine wine will be masked completely.

The next few pages consist of an introduction to those parts of chemistry which it is needful to know to have some understanding of the flavour of wine. They are necessarily elementary, and readers who have a working knowledge of chemistry can safely skim the theory bits. I have covered some of the ground in a previous book, *Appreciating Whisky*. Since the approach was well received by readers, I make no apology for adopting it in respect of wine. It seems probable that few of the readers of the present volume will have read the previous work, so some repetition may be permissible. And, though there is some crossover, the chemistry of wine is substantially different from that of whisky.

CHEMISTRY, ORGANIC CHEMISTRY AND BIOCHEMISTRY

The science of chemistry, like all other sciences, is made up of observations, concepts, theories and techniques. What follows is a summary only of a few of the results: that is, theories which are generally accepted and conclusions which may be regarded as established. As with most other sciences, it is possible to have some understanding based on an acquaintance merely with the results of several hundred years' work by a great many people, without knowing how those results were arrived at. This is a long way from a systematic grasp of the science, but better than nothing.

The central concepts of chemistry – which may, for our purposes, be taken as facts – are to do with what things are made of and how the basic parts combine to make different sorts of matter. Everyone knows about atoms: how they were thought to be the fundamental particles until it was found that they could be broken up to release huge amounts of energy. For our purposes, we can take atoms as fundamental, with the reservation that each atom is made up of a central nucleus round which whizz one or more electrons. The nucleus has a positive electrical charge and the electrons a negative charge. Atoms are very small: the dot at the end of this sentence is made up of several hundred million atoms.

Atoms vary in how they are made up: hydrogen has only one electron, carbon has six, nitrogen seven and oxygen eight. Depending on how they are constituted, atoms have different characteristics. There are around a hundred types of atom, each type being known as an element. All matter is made up of atoms of those hundred elements, usually in combination with other atoms of the same or other elements. Combinations of atoms are called molecules, and it is as molecules that we mostly experience atoms. Just about everything is made up of molecules. The writing on this page is made up of molecules; so is the page; so are you.

In conventional depictions, each atom is represented by a letter. Thus, for example, carbon is C, oxygen O, hydrogen H and nitrogen N. Some elements have two letters, as lead Pb, from the Latin *plumbum*, meaning lead. (This is necessary, for there are over a hundred compounds and only twenty-six letters.) Atoms differ in their propensity to combine with each other. This difference is expressed numerically as the valency of the atom. The number of atoms of a given element in any molecule is shown by a numeral at the bottom right of the relevant letter. Hydrogen has a valency of one, oxygen of two, carbon of four, which means that one carbon atom can combine with four hydrogen atoms or with two oxygen, yielding methane CH_4 and carbon dioxide CO_2 respectively. One oxygen can combine with two hydrogen, to produce a compound commonly known as water, or H_2O. This notation is known as the molecular formula. The proportions in which atoms combine are not invariable and some compounds are exceptions to the general rule – hence H_2O_2 (hydrogen peroxide), an unstable arrangement which, at the drop of a hat, will split to give water and a free oxygen atom. (The free oxygen atom is what makes hydrogen peroxide effective as a cleaning and bleaching agent.)

The properties of any compound depend not only on how many atoms of each element are combined in the molecule, but on how the atoms are arranged. Different arrangements of the same atoms can lead to wildly different properties, as will shortly become evident. It is therefore desirable to indicate in any molecular formula the way in which the different elements are combined. The use of letters and numerals as above is fine up to a point, but its inadequacies soon become apparent, especially as regards compounds which have the same numbers of elements in varying arrangements. By arranging the element-symbols (the letters) spatially, it is possible to show how the atoms are arranged in the molecule. Bonds between atoms are depicted by lines, hence water is shown as an oxygen atom with a hydrogen attached to either side of it:

$$H-O-H$$

and methane as a carbon with a hydrogen on each of its four prongs:

$$H-\overset{\displaystyle H}{\underset{\displaystyle H}{C}}-H$$

Ethane, the next-largest molecule in the series, is, like methane, an odourless gas. Its molecular formula is C_2H_6 and its arrangement is:

$$H-\overset{\displaystyle H}{\underset{\displaystyle H}{C}}-\overset{\displaystyle H}{\underset{\displaystyle H}{C}}-H$$

With larger organic molecules, it becomes impracticable to show all the carbon and hydrogen atoms so a convention is adopted in which lines are used and every line is assumed to have one carbon atom attached to each end of it. Each carbon atom is assumed to have a hydrogen atom attached to any of its four prongs which are not otherwise occupied.

Thus ethane is shown as a line with the two carbons, one at either end, six hydrogens, three attached to each carbon. Thus:

———

Propane, a hydrocarbon with three carbon atoms, is shown as two lines meeting at an oblique angle. It is assumed that there is a carbon at either end and at the intersection (see below).

Carbon atoms have very peculiar properties and are quite unlike any other kind of atom. Organic chemistry is the chemistry of the carbon atom in all its compound forms, of which there are millions. Since there are so many of these and they play such an important part in our lives, they warrant special attention. The chemistry of living things is organic chemistry, for all living things are made up of organic molecules. We are made of organic compounds and so are most of the things we taste and smell, so the chemistry of taste is organic chemistry. That is, it is about one lot of organic compounds reacting with another lot. The difference is that the first lot – us – is alive and the other, by and large, isn't. (There are exceptions: we eat oysters which are alive as we eat them, which some vegetarians find disgusting, but so are most fruits, though nobody seems to be disgusted at the idea of eating apples.)

The main difference between carbon atoms and other atoms is that carbon atoms show a strong propensity to join up with others of their sort. Thus molecules arise in the form of long chains and rings, and with the addition of each new link to the chain, a new compound is born which has properties entirely different from those which precede it in the chain, or those which follow it. The simplest compounds of carbon and hydrogen – the hydrocarbons – are the long chains which occur when carbon atoms are added to the methane–ethane series. Thus propane and butane – with which we are familiar in the form of bottled gas – are the next two in the series, having three and four carbon atoms respectively:

Propane is:

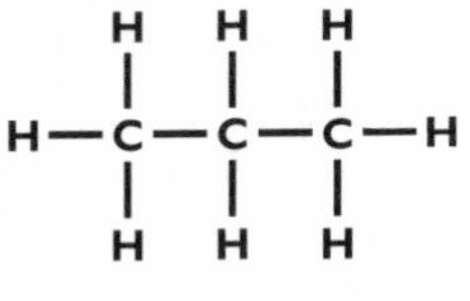

and the line formula is given above.

Butane is:

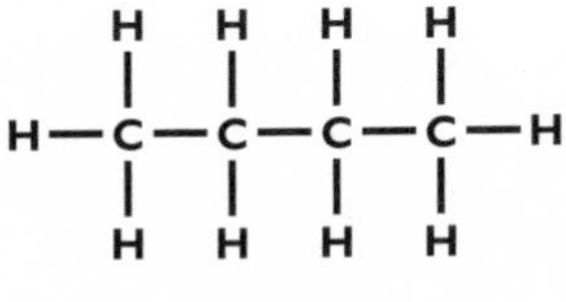

or in line formula:

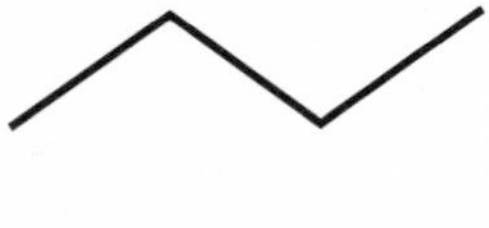

Methane, ethane, propane and butane are gases. Pentane, hexane and octane, which come next in the series, are liquids. We mostly experience these in the form of petrol and diesel fuel. As the chain gets longer, the substances get more dense and the heaviest hydrocarbons are solids such as paraffin wax, which you have probably used to light barbecues.

After carbon, by far the most common elements found in organic compounds are hydrogen, oxygen and nitrogen. Every variation in form or content of an organic molecule results in a compound with highly individual characteristics. For example, if we add one oxygen atom to methane (above), we get not a gas but a liquid, methyl alcohol:

$$H - \overset{\displaystyle \overset{H}{|}}{\underset{\displaystyle \underset{H}{|}}{C}} - OH$$

Methyl alcohol is the simplest in a series which contains a truly enormous number of compounds. Like the hydrocarbons, the longer the carbon chain, the heavier the molecule gets, and the more viscous the substance. Methyl alcohol is present in most wines, but in concentrations so low that it does no harm, despite being extremely poisonous. A single measure of the pure stuff will kill you, though, and much smaller doses will attack your optic nerve and blind you. In the 19th century, absinthe drinkers suffered from a condition which was later discovered to be methyl alcohol poisoning. Modern versions of absinthe use the aniseed flavourings characteristic of absinthe, but omit the methyl alcohol. Methyl alcohol is known as methylated spirit and used as a domestic solvent, in which form it is sold coloured purple and spiked with the odour of rats' urine, which most folk find unappetising.

All the alcohols are characterised by the possession of the –OH group. Thus ethyl alcohol, the next one up the chain, is C_2H_5OH:

$$H - \overset{\displaystyle \overset{H}{|}}{\underset{\displaystyle \underset{H}{|}}{C}} - \overset{\displaystyle \overset{H}{|}}{\underset{\displaystyle \underset{H}{|}}{C}} - OH$$

This is the alcohol principally present in wine. It is heavier than methyl, not so poisonous and not so volatile. The longer the carbon chain gets, the heavier and more viscous the alcohol. By the time we get to amyl and hexyl alcohols, the fluids are beginning to look like oils. Indeed, in wine making they and other even higher alcohols are known as fusel oils. If present in infinitesimally small quantities, they make a significant contribution to the flavour of some wines – but above a low threshold fusel oils are considered as off-odours. The exception to this is port wine, in which the high levels of fusel oils contributed by the grape spirit with which the wine is fortified are considered to be desirable.

Also known as ethanol, ethyl alcohol is the substance which we usually refer to as alcohol, since it is the alcohol we normally encounter in our drinks. The term comes from the Arabic *al kuhl*. This phrase originally meant the fine powder, antimony sulphide, used to darken the eyelids to make the wearer more alluring to the members of the opposite (or in some cases, the same) sex. (I bet you thought there would be no sex in a chapter on chemistry. You were wrong.) Anyway, these Arabs – chaps, mostly – thought pretty highly of the stuff they put on their eyes. It seems they thought it the very essence of sexuality: so much so that the phrase came to be used to refer to the essence of just about anything. It is a short step to the application of the term to distillate, given that the Arabs invented perfume as we know it and they used distillation to extract essential oils from flowers.

The -OH group, known as a hydroxyl group, which characterises alcohols, is significant in matters of taste, for compounds in which it is present are mostly perceived as sweet. True, ethanol itself doesn't taste very sweet, but if another hydroxyl is added to the molecule it becomes ethanediol, which does. This compound is also known as ethylene glycol. Its molecular formula is $C_2H_6O_2$.

Ethylene glycol mixes readily with water and, when it does, it prevents the water freezing until its temperature is well below the usual freezing point. Despite its close similarity to alcohol, ethylene glycol is seriously toxic and a small amount will kill you.

Ethylene glycol is very close to glycerol, $C_3H_8O_3$, which also is sweet and won't do you any harm at all. It occurs naturally in lots of foods and drinks and is widely used in the processed-food industry, where it is valued because it makes food pleasanter to eat. This it does by making the food feel smoother in the mouth.

Glycerol occurs naturally in wines and is considered highly desirable, for not only does it add a little sweetness, but its viscosity makes the wine, as with food, feel smooth in the mouth. When we refer to a wine as being smooth, it is generally glycerol which gives us that impression. When, after you have swirled the wine, you see legs on the glass (see below), you are seeing glycerol. Having a longer chain than ethanol, the glycerol is more viscous and takes longer to detach itself from the glass than either the alcohol or the water in the wine. Glycerol is found in both red and white wines, but is most noticeable in very sweet whites such as Sauternes, which have lots of it. (The noble rot, *Botrytis cinerea*, concentrates the glycerol in the grapes as well as the sugars; see page 92.)

Glycerol, being a simple compound with such desirable properties, is sometimes added to wines with the object of improving their flavour and mouth feel. This is illegal in most wine-producing countries, but is known to occur. The great Austrian wine scandal of 1985 arose when some unscrupulous individuals added an industrial solvent to some white wines, with the intention of making them sweeter and smoother. They presumably thought they were adding glycerol but in fact added diethylene glycol, which is ethylene glycol's big brother and even more toxic. The consequences were devastating: exports of Austrian wines the following year were down by four-fifths and Austria's wines have suffered ever since in the perception of the international public.

As hydroxyl groups are added to the molecule, sweetness increases. If you have a molecule consisting of six carbons and five hydroxyl groups, you get sugar, which isn't toxic except in high concentrations. (Jams preserve fruit because they contain sugars at concentrations high enough to be toxic to the bacteria and moulds which otherwise would consume the fruits and cause their decay.)

Glucose is $C_6H_{12}O_6$ a nd in line formula it looks like this:

Glucose also exists in the form of a closed ring of five carbon atoms with one oxygen, as shown at the top of page 51.

The same lot of atoms – $C_6H_{12}O_6$ – in a mirror-image arrangement is fructose, which is even sweeter than glucose. Both combine readily with oxygen – burn – to form carbon dioxide and water and give off energy. Both are also highly soluble in water and it is the combination of those two attributes that enables them to constitute the energy source of all living things. Being soluble, they can be transported between cells and within them; being capable of oxidisation, they act as fuel. Glucose is the form in which energy is stored by plants, the energy of sunlight being used to synthesise sugars from water and carbon dioxide.

All life on this planet is involved with sugar in one way or another: we and our wines are an example. Plants absorb the energy of sunlight and store it by using it to combine inorganic compounds, water (H_2O) and carbon dioxide (CO_2), to produce the organic compound sugar and oxygen gas – a process known as photosynthesis; the sugar they use to build their bodies (see below) and to power their growth and reproduction. Plants store their sugars in various ways and all fruits come complete with an energy store to fuel the growth of the new plant. In the case of the grapevine, the energy store is the sugars in the grape.

Glucose and fructose molecules have the ability to join together – a process known as polymerisation – to form sucrose and maltose, types of molecules known as disaccharides. Sucrose is the form of sugar used in the kitchen. It isn't as sweet as glucose or fructose and is mostly obtained from sugar cane or beets. As with hydrocarbon chains, the combination process can go on and on, building polymers which consist of ever-longer chains of glucose and fructose molecules, known generically as polysaccharides. Starch is a polysaccharide. Some plants, such as vines, beets, fruits and sugar canes, store their energy directly as sugars, but most do so as starches: cereals and root crops such as wheat and potatoes contain their energy in the form of starch. When we eat starchy foods, our digestion breaks down the starch molecules into their constituent sugars. If we consume more than we burn, our system stores the excess as fat. The only way of getting rid of fat is either to increase the amount we burn, or to reduce our intake below our existing burn rate. The reason why most diets don't work is that they ignore or try to evade this simple logic. Unfortunately for obese people, the human metabolism is very efficient as an energy converter, so you have to take a huge amount of exercise to get rid of a tiny amount of fat.

Not only do plants use polysaccharides as energy stores, they use them as the structural materials of the plants themselves. In chains even longer than those of starches, polysaccharides become cellulose, which is the woody material of which all plants are made. Wood itself is mainly lignin, a form of cellulose. Thus the oak or chestnut cask in which your wine is matured is ultimately made of the same stuff as the grape from which the wine came. When we understand that, we begin to get a handle on the processes by which the use of wood can affect the flavour of wine.

Plants also use fats and oils as energy stores. The oil in the olive is there as a source of energy for the germinating olive tree. The oil in a corn cob acts as a potential source of fuel, in addition to the sugars and starches. Oils and fats are long chains or rings (or both) of carbon, hydrogen and oxygen, whose prototype is the glycerol mentioned above.

Unlike plants which must synthesise their energy source using sunlight, animals get their energy ready-made by consuming plants or other animals. They convert the fats, oils and starches they ingest into sugars. They fuel their activities by burning those sugars, combining them with the oxygen which plants have released into the air and giving off carbon dioxide, thus completing the cycle. When we eat the grape, we do so in order that its sugars may eventually provide us with a source of power. The petrol and diesel fuel we use to power our motor vehicles are not very different in content or structure from the fat we burn (or hope to burn) when we exercise – which isn't so surprising, when you consider that they are the fossilised remains of plants which hundreds of millions of years ago used the sun's light to synthesise hydrocarbons from carbon dioxide and water. Motor vehicle engines, like humans, produce carbon dioxide as a by-product of their energy production.

The conversion by plants and animals of polysaccharides into useable sugars takes us neatly into the realm of biochemistry. Biochemistry is the chemistry of living things: it differs from organic chemistry in that, although all the compounds with which biochemistry deals are organic compounds, not all organic compounds are biochemical ones. (One of the most important events in the history of chemistry was when, in 1828, the German chemist Freidrich Wohler accidentally synthesised urea, a simple organic compound, from inorganic materials, thus putting paid to the then-current theory that what distinguished living things from inanimate ones was a mysterious vital force.)

The science of biochemistry is particularly applicable to wine making, for the processes by which grapes become wines are biochemical ones. Indeed the father of biochemistry, in most people's opinion, is Louis Pasteur, the great French chemist who in the mid-1850s showed that the process of fermentation by which the sugars in grapes are converted to alcohol comes about because of the metabolism of living organisms, namely yeasts. We now know of Pasteur mainly because his name has entered the language via the term 'pasteurisation'. Pasteur was interested not only in the processes by which grapes become good wines, but also in what makes wines go bad. He correctly identified the culprits in the latter case as microorganisms and suggested that they might be killed by heating. By heating wine beyond a given temperature, he was able to kill off bacteria such as *Acetobacter*, which turns the alcohol in wine into acetic acid – which we know as vinegar. (Indeed, the word 'vinegar' comes from the French *vin aigre*, or spoiled wine. Wine vinegar is made simply by encouraging rather than preventing this process.) There were few things the French in the mid-19th century thought more important than wine going off, but tuberculosis was one of them, for the disease was widespread and incurable. As a result of Pasteur's work, the tuberculin bacillus was identified and milk was discovered to be one of its main vectors. Medical science was still unable to cure the disease (even today it is very difficult) but at least it was possible to stop people getting it in the first place by heating the milk sufficiently to kill the bacillus. Most milk today is pasteurised, so that we won't catch tuberculosis. The milk may have lost some of its flavour, but that's preferable to coughing your lungs up.

We shall return to pasteurisation and the things which spoil wine later. For the moment, we should note that a large part of biochemistry has to do with the operations of enzymes. In inorganic as in organic chemistry, many chemical reactions are brought about by the presence of catalysts. The catalytic converter in your car exhaust turns unburnt fuel into harmless carbon dioxide and water. It can do so because it contains a catalyst which, while it makes the reaction happen, is not itself consumed in the reaction and so continues to be available – unless, that is, it gets fouled up, which is what happens when you use a leaded fuel by mistake for an unleaded. The lead reacts with the catalyst, renders it useless, and you have to shell out for a new exhaust next time your car goes in for a service.)

Enzymes are organic catalysts. They are proteins whose sole purpose is to facilitate the reactions which take place within the cell. Each cell in a plant or an animal has a finite lifespan, so it has only a limited time in which to do all the things it needs to do, for the organism of which it is a part to function. Enzymes make reactions happen millions of times faster than otherwise they would – and they make them happen at temperatures much lower than would otherwise be required. The cell – plant or animal – creates these proteins for the express purpose of facilitating its reactions and each enzyme usually has one and only one specific reaction to deal with. The science of enzymes is large and complex and we must content ourselves here with only the most general description.

When the sunshine turns some of the acids in a grape into sugars and makes it sweet, enzymes are at work. When the yeast in the vat converts those sugars into alcohol, it's the same thing, only different enzymes. When we drink the alcohol and it makes us drunk, enzymes have been at work. When through inebriation we get into bed with someone whom we would otherwise regard as quite unsuitable, enzymes are to blame. The list is endless. All life depends on enzymes.

SWEETNESS

When a wine tastes sweet, its flavour is almost entirely down to the presence of glucose and fructose in the wine. There are other factors: alcohol contributes to the impression of sweetness, as do glycerol and certain other, sweet-associated flavours such as floweriness and fruitiness. But the most important cause by far is what is known in the trade as residual sugar. This is sugar which was present before fermentation began and which remains after fermentation has ceased. Even dry wines have some sugar left in them and sweet wines have lots.

As we have said above, yeast is a living organism which (as it were) eats sugar and excretes alcohol. There are lots of different sorts of yeast which are used to convert the sugars in grapes into alcohol, some of them occurring naturally on the skins of the grapes, others artificially cultured and introduced by the wine maker. They vary a lot in their tolerance of different conditions. The proportion of the available sugars a yeast is able to convert into alcohol depends on many factors. If there is a lot of sugar to begin with, so much alcohol may be produced that the yeast is poisoned by the alcohol well before it has converted all the sugar. Since some yeasts – like some folk – can stand more alcohol than others, it stands to reason that a weak yeast with a little sugar and a strong yeast with a lot of sugar may leave the same amount of sugar unfermented. The difference will be that in the latter case the alcohol content of the wine will be much higher.

When a substantial amount of sugar is left in the wine there is a danger that a secondary fermentation may take place once the wine is bottled. Secondary fermentation alone is not too much of a problem, provided the only noticeable result is the production of more alcohol and carbon dioxide, and a diminution of the sweetness of the wine caused by the sugar being used up. But the conditions which lead to an unintended alcoholic fermentation may also produce other, less desirable effects, such as bacterial fermentation to produce acetic acid, in which case the wine becomes vinegary as well as fizzy. Secondary fermentation can be controlled, though, which is what happens in making sparkling wine. The wine is first filtered to remove any yeasts, perhaps pasteurised, and then bottled under sterile conditions, so that no wild yeasts or bacteria can get in. Sugar and yeast are then added and the carbon dioxide produced in the resultant fermentation, being unable to escape, is forced to dissolve in the wine, in which it creates a considerable gas pressure. As soon as the bottle is opened, the carbon dioxide escapes, which is what creates the fizz.

SOURNESS

Things taste sour because they contain acids. All acids taste sour: organic and inorganic alike. (I was once foolish enough to put a finger in my mouth after having spilt some battery acid on it. I can tell you, sulphuric acid, even diluted, tastes very sour indeed.) Almost all the acids we meet in our food and drink are organic acids – though there are a few exceptions such as the phosphoric and carbonic acids used to flavour some sweet drinks such as cola. The strong sensation produced in the mouth by acids is thought to be due to the presence of free hydrogen ions (positively charged hydrogen atoms) which combine with negatively charged components of some of the proteins in the taste buds of the mouth. The combination causes a change in the shape of the protein molecules, which triggers an electrical impulse in the nerve endings, which is relayed to the brain, whence it registers in our consciousness as the sensation of sourness.

The acid which derives from ethanol is acetic acid, $C_2H_4O_2$ or, as it is sometimes described, CH_3COOH:

The -OOH ending of the molecule is characteristic of acids generally, and is to be found in all the organic acids.

Two sorts of acidity are to be found in wines, described as fixed and volatile acidity. Volatile acidity is so called because it can be removed by steam distillation. The phrase refers mainly to acetic acid, though traces of a few other volatile acids such as lactic and succinic acids are to be found in wines. Acetic acid comes about when ethanol is oxidised, oxygen being necessary for the growth of the *Acetobacter* bacterium, whose metabolic processes are the most usual cause of acetic acid in wine. We owe our understanding of acetic acid in wine to (again) Louis Pasteur. Pasteur had been asked to investigate why so many casks of Burgundy shipped to England had become vinegary: his conclusion, that acetic acid production is the result of the metabolic processes of a microorganism, not only answered the question, but laid the foundation of biochemistry.

Volatile acidity shows itself in the aroma of wine: not, as you might expect, as the smell of vinegar, but as the odour of pear drops or glue. The concentration of acetic acid is much lower than it is in vinegar and not easily detected in an oxidised wine. But acetic acid reacts with the ethyl alcohol in wine to form an ester, ethyl acetate (see below). Since the threshold of recognition of ethyl acetate is about 100 times lower than our threshold for acetic acid, it is the ester we detect. At very low levels ethyl acetate is acceptable and contributes to an overall pleasing bouquet, but above a very low threshold it becomes very noticeable and spoils the aroma and flavour of wine. The exception to this rule is in the case of some swanky Sauternes, in which pronounced ethyl acetate is considered acceptable.

Just as acetic acid is created by the oxidation of ethyl alcohol, so the higher alcohols oxidise to the corresponding acids, known as fatty acids. None of these smell nice, and some are very nasty indeed. Propionic acid smells of rancid butter and a number of the higher acids have a goaty odour. However, fatty acids can be important contributors to the bouquet of a wine. Remember we said that sometimes a faint whiff of a foul smell can be pleasing: fatty acids have that effect in wine aroma. At or just below the threshold of perception, some fatty acids can contribute that indefinable something, hovering on the brink between nice and nasty, which makes a wine not only interesting but perfectly delicious. In evolutionary terms, this probably has its origins in sex. As we all know, sex can be a smelly business at times. Perfumes are often delicious and their smell can be mildly aphrodisiacal. But the whiff of a sweaty armpit or a bodily secretion just at the threshold and beneath the perfume will do all that smell can do for a person. If the odour rises much above threshold level, it becomes counterproductive and can be disgusting – though the latter depends on one's state of arousal, for our olfactory perceptions are influenced by our hormonal chemistry. The same holds true of wines. The Montrachet we had at lunch today has just a trace of funkiness, which makes it perfectly delicious. More, and it would be revolting; less and it would be a lesser wine. The wine drunk by two diners, whose dinner is the prelude to bed, tastes quite different from the same wine the morning after.

The fixed acids are those which contribute most positively to the flavours of wines. By far the most important are malic acid and tartaric acid, both of which occur naturally in the grape. In the unripe grape, malic acid predominates, but as the grape ripens the sharp-tasting malic acid is converted to the milder tartaric. Both acids are made up of carbon, hydrogen and oxygen atoms. The difference between them consists only of the substitution of an OH group for one of the hydrogen atoms attached to a carbon.

Malic acid is so-named from the Latin *malus*, meaning 'apple'. When you bite into a Granny Smith, the ferociously sour taste is caused by malic acid. If the apple is left on the tree until it is almost ready to drop, you will find the apple much less sour, its acids having been converted into sugars.

Similarly, as the grape ripens, not only does some of the malic acid convert to tartaric acid, but some is changed into sugars. Since our tolerance of sourness is modified by sweetness, the resultant wine may be acceptable as regards its acidity. For many red wines, however, the wine is still too sharp and yet another process is required. This is known as the malolactic fermentation. It is a secondary fermentation quite different from that described above: it usually occurs in the winery, not in the bottle. Pasteur had a long look at it but couldn't figure out how it worked. Indeed, its mechanism was not understood until the middle of the 20th century, when French biochemists in Bordeaux and Burgundy discovered that it was brought about by a bacterium called *Lactobacillus* and one or two of its relatives.

The malic acid molecule loses a carbon and two oxygens to become lactic acid:

$$O=\overset{\displaystyle OH}{\overset{|}{C}} - \overset{\displaystyle OH}{\overset{|}{C}} - \overset{\displaystyle H}{\underset{\underset{\displaystyle H}{|}}{\overset{|}{C}}} - H$$

The lactic acid produced by malolactic fermentation is much less acidic than malic acid. Lactic acid is so called because it is the acid which occurs in milk. Because lactic has replaced malic acid, the wine tastes less sour. Since most people prefer red wines to have a lower acidity than white, it is in red wine making that malolactic fermentation is most commonly employed. There is a danger with white wines that the reduction in acidity produced by malolactic fermentation will leave them with insufficient acidity and they will turn out flaccid. Only in the case of white wines made from grapes such as Chardonnay, where there is a high enough acid level to start with, and the finished wine is required to be soft and fruity, is malolactic fermentation desirable.

The malolactic bacteria – *Lactobacillus*, *Pediococcus*, *Leuconostoc* and others – are often present naturally in the grape must (the juice being made into wine). They like warmth and they don't like sulphur dioxide, so if malolactic fermentation is not desired, the best course is to keep the wine cool and to add sulphur dioxide.

Besides the softening of the wine brought about by malolactic fermentation, there are other consequences which may or may not be desirable. Some of the fruit flavour may be lost, as esters are broken down. This may be balanced by a gain in a buttery flavour, caused by the presence of diacetyl. A small amount of the latter is good, but our threshold for diacetyl is pretty low and few folk want their wines to have lashings of butter.

Tartaric acid is at least as important a component of the flavour of wine as malic acid. In view of what has been said so far, it will come as no surprise to the reader that the chemical similarity of the two acids does not have a correlate in their properties. Malic acid is a common acid and is found in many fruits. Tartaric acid is a component of many fruits, but is very rarely present at the levels it reaches in grapes. (This is very convenient for archaeologists: so rare is tartaric acid that its remains in ceramic containers can be taken as a sure sign of wine making.)

$$\begin{array}{ccc} \text{OH} & \text{OH} \\ | & | \\ \text{H} - \text{C} - \text{C} - \text{H} \\ | & | \\ \text{HOOC} & \text{COOH} \end{array}$$

Tartaric acid is present in the grape from an early stage of its development and the concentration of the acid does not alter appreciably with ripeness. It is present both as the acid and as a salt, in both grapes and wine. A salt is formed when an acid combines with a mineral. The two most common minerals in wine are potassium and calcium. Both combine with tartaric acid to form potassium and calcium tartrates. The salts are much less soluble in wine than the acid itself. As wine ages in cask or in bottle, tartrates reach levels at which they can no longer remain in solution and they precipitate out as crystals. In white wine, those crystals look exactly like shards of glass and diners who don't know any better have been known to reject wines on that ground. In red, the precipitate tends to be brown-coloured, in which case it is usually acceptable as a sediment, which is thought to be less offensive. In neither case does it matter in the slightest, so it's a good idea to familiarise oneself with the stuff in the bottom of the bottle before making a fuss.

The salts of tartaric acid do not have any influence on the flavour of a wine (they don't taste sour), so the tendency of the acid to form salts acts as a limit on the acidity deriving from tartaric acid. Thus the variation in tartaric acid levels between different varieties of grape (Pinot Noir and Malbec are low; Palomino high) tends to level out.

The tendency of tartaric acid and mineral tartrates to crystallise causes vessels in which wine is fermented and matured to become covered in thick deposits. So large are these that they require to be removed periodically and, since any chemical method of doing so would render the vessel useless for making or storing wine, this must be done by hand, with adze and chipping hammer. The quantities of tartaric acid and tartrate crystals so obtained are large enough for wine making to form the principal source of industrial tartrates.

The formation of tartrate crystals poses a problem for all wine bottlers. A filter will remove any crystals present in the wine, but it cannot remove dissolved tartaric acid or tartrates. Most liquids will dissolve more when warm than they will when cold and if the wine has been filtered when warm and is then stored in a cool place, dissolved tartrates may crystallise out. The only way to prevent this is to cool the wine and hold it at a low temperature for long enough for all of the tartrates to precipitate – usually two or three weeks – then to bring the wine back to cellar temperature. This tends to be very effective. Even so, it is still quite common to find crystalline deposits in wine, especially in white German wines, which, because they are made in a cool climate, have higher levels of tartaric acid than any other wines.

We have described the three main acids to be found in wine. There are, of course, lots more – the deeper you look, the more you find – of which the most important is succinic acid. This acid occurs naturally in the grape, and is also a by-product of yeast metabolism in fermentation. It is not as tart as either malic or tartaric acids, but in some wines contributes in a small way to the overall acidity and flavour. It reacts with ethyl alcohol to form esters, which may contribute to the aroma of certain wines, but it is unlikely that you will detect the influence, given that it is slight compared to other, more powerful flavours.

At this point we ought to mention the pH scale, by which acids are measured and which is sometimes referred to in books about wines. This yardstick is often confusing to non-scientists, for it is counter-intuitive. We can easily indicate the strength of, say, tartaric acid in a wine, by telling how many grams of acid are present per litre of wine. The larger the number of grams per litre, the more acid the wine. However, pH doesn't work that way. It is a scale, from 0 to 14, with the strongest acid (sulphuric acid) scoring 0 and the strongest alkali (sodium hydroxide) 14. The scale is not linear but logarithmic – which means that whole numbers differ by a factor of 10 – so an acid with a pH of 2 is ten times as strong as one which has a pH of 3, and so on. It's a crazy system, but one which has been around for a long time and one which scientists seem to find useful, so we have to put up with it. At least the neutral point is logical: 7 is the pH of pure water, which is neither acid nor alkaline. Wines measured on the pH scale run from a very sour 2.9 to a pretty flaccid 4.2. The best wines are usually around 3.2 to 3.5, the ideal depending on a lot of other factors, such as sweetness.

Acids can affect the colour and the aroma of wines. They help maintain the colour of wines: anthocyanins (see below) progressively lose their colour as acidity declines, so good acidity to start with is desirable. Wines of low pH (i.e. acidic wines) are less susceptible to oxidation than those of higher: as acidity diminishes, wines lose their freshness and begin to show signs of oxidation products such as aldehydes.

BITTERNESS

Most supermarkets these days sell at least two sorts of grapes: green and black. The black are usually cheaper than the green, especially if the green are of the seedless variety. Black grapes are much more bitter than green ones and most people don't like them as much and won't pay so much for them. If, like me, you are partial to black grapes, which taste differently from green ones, you must either put up with the bitter taste, or else spit out both seeds and skins. I hate the inconvenience of having to spit things out and long ago accustomed myself to eating various sorts of food entire. Prawns, for example, are a pest to peel. Their shells don't taste of anything and if you eat them entire, you soon get used to the texture. The same is true of green grapes: if you eat the seeds and skins, they are a bit crunchy and taste just fine. But I draw the line at eating black grapes whole: they are just too bitter. The bitterness in black grapes is due to a large group of compounds normally referred to as tannins – though, strictly speaking, true tannins are minority members of the group known as phenols, which is where we begin this section.

Phenols resemble alcohols, in that they are hydrocarbons which have a hydroxyl (OH) group attached to one of the carbons. Where they differ hugely from the hydrocarbon chain molecules is in the arrangement of the carbons, which, instead of being strung together in a line, are arranged in a ring. As you might expect by now, any variation, even in the shape of a molecule, will make for a big difference in its properties. The basic molecule in this series is benzene, C_6H_6.

This is a very important molecule, and all sorts of interesting things are based on it. It is called a cyclic compound, because the carbon atoms are arranged in a ring. There are lots of these cyclic compounds, running from three carbons in a triangle upward. However, five- and six-carbon rings are much the most common. Here we are concerned mainly with the six-member rings, beginning with benzene. Benzene is a rather pleasant smelling liquid, like a cross between petrol and disinfectant. Indeed it was used as an additive to petrol until quite recently, but was discovered to be

carcinogenic and to have killed a lot of petrol-pump attendants.
Many of the variations on benzene are smelly, some nicely so, some
not. So they are collectively termed aromatic compounds. (This is a
bit misleading: 'aromatic' in common parlance means smelling nice,
and some of these don't. However, chemists are good at chemistry
and not necessarily at language, so they can be forgiven if the
terminology isn't always all it might be.)

Benzene, like the straight-line carbon/hydrogen compounds, can
add on all sorts of atoms and molecules and, as you might expect,
with each little change comes a big change in characteristics. To
name but a few: if you add two little side chains to this petroleum-
smelling compound, you get limonene, which makes lemons smell as
they do; add a few carbons, hydrogens and oxygens, and you get the
compounds which smell of jasmine, spearmint, menthol, cinnamon,
cloves, geraniums, aniseed, camphor, vanilla, nutmeg, violets,
raspberries and a hundred others. All made of the same stuff in very
similar arrangements. A really good, trained and practised nose can
detect a lot of these flavour compounds at very low densities – so
don't be surprised if someone who knows his or her business can
detect all sorts of stuff in a glass of good wine.

There is a truly vast number of possible compounds using the
benzene ring, either together with other rings or in connection with
straight-line compounds, and just about every variation in between.
Some of them are mind-bogglingly complex and one can only
speculate as to the effort involved in working out their composition
and structure. We shall content ourselves with looking at a few
which are of relevance to the flavour of wine. For our present
purposes we are interested in phenols. If you add a hydroxyl (OH)
group to a benzene ring, you get C_6H_5OH. Despite the presence of
the hydroxyl group, phenols do not have the characteristics of
alcohols. They have other properties, though, which are highly
relevant to wines. Phenolic compounds are responsible for a large
part of the flavour of wines, for most of their colour and for many of

the most important changes which take place as wine ages in the cellar. They affect how the wines feel in the mouth and how they smell. They are responsible for many of the anti-microbial properties of wines.

The structure of phenol is as follows:

Phenolic compounds are to be found in the grapes themselves (in the seeds and skins especially), they are produced by yeast metabolism, and they are extracted from the wood in which wines are fermented and matured. So it will be seen that phenolic flavour compounds may arise at any stage in the production and maturation of wine – and even after the wine is made and in bottle, many of the changes which take place with age are the result of alterations in the structure of phenolic compounds.

We experience the flavour of phenolics primarily as tannins: the bitter, astringent sensation in the mouth which we get with stewed tea or unsweetened, stewed rhubarb. Tannins are very complex polymers of the phenol molecule. You will recall that the simple glucose ring was capable of all sorts of strange effects when two or more rings were joined together, with or without the presence of add-ons in the form of side chains. The same is true of the phenols, and the tannins are made up of several benzene rings, each with two or more hydroxyl groups attached and carbon, hydrogen and oxygen atoms stuck on in various ways. If you think that's bad, you should see some of the big ones. The larger molecules tend to be those which cause astringent sensations.

Besides the primary, bitter flavours which derive from phenolics, there is also the range of secondary flavours which results from the formation of compounds allied to those described above in relation to benzene. There are thousands of such compounds, which may derive, like the tannins, either from the wine or from the wood. Vanillin, $C_8H_8O_3$, (illustrated at the top of page 64) is one of the simpler.

The favour of vanilla is an important component of many wines, even though present in very small amounts. It is a breakdown product of the oak wood and is often to be found alongside tannic flavour, which it modifies to advantage. One thinks here of some heavily oaked Chardonnays, which without the vanilla would not be palatable.

Besides their role in flavour, phenols are also important in the colour of wines. While, strictly speaking, colour lies outside our remit, we should consider it, for colour can sometimes (not always) be taken as an indicator of flavour.

Both white and red wines derive their colour from phenolic compounds. Black grapes contain much higher levels of phenolic compounds than do green. White wines derive their yellow colour inthe first instance from the phenolics in the skin and stems of the grapes used; the colour deepens as the colour compounds oxidise and polymerise. As white wines age, the colour often deepens as this process continues in the bottle, to the point at which, with a very old wine, there is a convergence of colour between white and red: the white darkening as the red gets lighter and more yellow.

White wines are often made using black grapes: the grapes are quickly crushed and pressed and the must is allowed as little contact with the skins as possible. The Pinot Noir which is used to make Champagne is an example. The colour of red wines comes from a group of phenolic compounds called anthocyanins. There is little correlation between the presence of tannins and that of anthocyanins. Pinot Noir, Cabernet Sauvignon, Syrah, Gamay Noir, Malbec and Tempranillo grapes all have high levels of total phenolics, but the level of anthocyanins in Pinot Noir and Malbec is quite low. While white wine grapes such as Chardonnay, Grenache and Sauvignon Blanc all have highish levels of phenolics (though nothing near as high as the black grapes), they have either low or non-existent levels of anthocyanins.

Anthocyanins are responsible for the colours of many fruits and flowers. Cyanidin and delphinidin give their blue colours to cornflowers and delphiniums, respectively. Peonidin, petunidin and malvidin are all closely related compounds which cause the coloration of peonies, petunias and mallows. All consist of three connected benzene-type rings, with hydroxyl and glucose molecules attached. Thus the colour of wines is caused by these same three sorts of atom: carbon, hydrogen and oxygen, which make up sugars and alcohols.

The depth and nature of the colour depend on many factors: the variety of the vine, the ripeness of the grape, the weather, the date of the harvest, the length and the temperature of the maceration of the skins in the new wine, the acidity of the grape juice and the amount of sulphur dioxide used. Anthocyanins can cause both red and blue coloration. A young red wine can vary in colour from blue–black to pale crimson, depending on which anthocyanins are present and the concentrations of each.

As red wines age, the anthocyanin molecules oxidise and polymerise and combine with tannins and other phenolics. As the molecule size increases, the colouring becomes progressively less soluble in alcohol and water, and eventually precipitates out of solution; hence, both the diminution of the colour of old red wines and the presence of sediment in the bottle. The colour tends to change from the dark purple of young, highly pigmented reds, to the biscuit yellow of very old red wines.

It is now pretty well accepted that the phenols found in red wine are good for you. Some of the polyphenols in red wines are antioxidants and there is speculation that, because the ageing process in the body is in part due to oxidation, red wines may be beneficial from that point of view. Other polyphenols appear to impede the agglomeration of platelets in the blood and are therefore effective in combating coronary heart disease. Red wine has long been recognised as having anti-microbial properties. It protects against gastrointestinal diseases of various sorts, mostly those caused by microorganisms in drinking water. Fortunately, the phenols in red wine do not have the same effect on the growth and functioning of yeasts and lactic acid bacteria. They do, however, impede the secondary bacterial fermentation which produces the carbon dioxide in bottled sparkling wines – which is why almost all sparkling wines are white.

FLAVOUR ORIGINS
≈SMELL≈

We now come to that group of flavours – by far the larger – which we get by smell rather than by taste. It is perfectly possible to produce a wine which has exactly the right levels and balance of sweetness, acidity and (maybe) tannins, but which nobody would rate as a wine of any quality. Many of the white wines of northern Italy made from the Trebbiano grape varietal fall into this class: they are wines for drinking as a substitute for water to quench a thirst, not wines to be savoured for their flavour. (It is easy to criticise them on this ground – and they are often criticised – but the condemnation is misplaced.) As such, they do not require to have high levels of flavour and the people who drink them locally do not expect them to have. The Soaves of this world will do very nicely to illustrate the message of this next section: that almost all the flavours we value in a fine wine derive from smell rather than taste. All the subtlety and delight, the interest and the mystery depend on the appeal to the nose.

FRUIT AND FLOWER AROMAS

Every wine drinker is familiar with the fruity, flowery flavours which are so often the first impression of a wine – be it the blackcurrants and raspberries of a young Cabernet Sauvignon, or the elderflower and lychees of a Riesling or a Gewürztraminer. The variety of fruit and flower flavours found in wine is enormous and difficult to classify, and there is a lot of crossover, hence the decision in this section to discuss fruity and flowery aromas together. It will be apparent from the Aroma Wheel (see page 27) that while there are six subdivisions of fruity flavours, there are none for flowery aromas. Flowery fragrances are more difficult to identify in the first place (with certain exceptions), there is a huge number of flower odours, each of which differs only very slightly from a number of others, and the organoleptic classification of flower fragrances is problematical and subjective. The five examples given on the Aroma Wheel under the classification Floral – linalool, orange blossom, rose, violet and geranium – are all aromas which are relatively easy to disassociate, although, as will be seen, chemically they can be pretty close.

Linalool is classed as a flowery fragrance, though it has elements of fruit about it. It is the flowery, citrus aroma which you find in Riesling, Muscat and Gewürztraminer wines. It is difficult to describe exactly and there is no single fruit or flower to which one can point, and say, 'That's it', hence the proper name rather than some class of fragrance such as 'rose'. Its closest match in the world of flowers is the elusive scent of the iris.

Chemically, linalool is a terpene. Terpenes are a class of compounds of carbon, hydrogen and oxygen whose basic unit is isoprene, C_5H_8. This is the five-carbon unit which is the monomer of rubber (i.e. rubbers are made up mainly of lots of isoprene units strung together).

Terpenes string the isoprene units together, but in a way slightly different from the method which gets us rubber. Terpenes are common in many plants, in which they produce both colour and fragrance – not something one would expect of bits of rubber strung together – but by now you will have got used to the bizarre consequences of the slightest changes in organic molecules.

Terpenes are also responsible for the scents of roses and geraniums, so figure largely in the flowery flavours of wines. Geraniol, $C_{10}H_{18}O$, is a terpene molecule and an important constituent of both rose and geraniums. Geraniol has an –OH group, which makes it a cousin of the alcohols. (Roses also owe their fragrance to B-damascenone, which is a ketone.) Terpenes occur naturally in the ripening grape, and are what gives the aromatic muscat grape most of its flavour. The grape is not the only possible source of terpenes, however, for it appears that terpenes form in wines during ageing; terpenes which are bound to sugars are released and become olfactorily active.

Terpenes are to be found mostly in white wines, much less in red. However, in whites they show themselves in all sorts of ways. Very small changes in the terpene structure can produce scents as different as pinewood and violets. The scent of violets is caused by ionone, $C_{13}H_{20}O$, which as you can see is made up again of the same stuff, just slightly differently arranged.

The intermediate divisions of the fruity flavours are relatively easy to comprehend. We are all familiar with the smell of citrus fruits, which are quite unlike any others. Grapefruit and lemon are the only two members of the citrus family listed because they are the only citrus aromas commonly found in wines. Both fruits contain citric acid, which is a simple acid, $C_6H_8O_7$, which is very close to many of the compounds we have been discussing. Before we begin to look at fruit flavours, however, we ought to say a few words about esters.

Esters are a very important in fruit flavours. They are typically formed when an acid meets an alcohol. (As above, when acetic acid meets ethanol to produce ethyl acetate, the perceptible aroma of wine which has gone off because of *Acetobacter* fermentation.) More than one hundred and sixty esters have been identified in wine, though only a few at levels high enough to be perceptible. However, those that are, are important, though, especially with regard to the flavour of young white wines.

Esters can be formed from straight-chain or cyclic compounds. With very few and unimportant exceptions, the latter do not figure at levels high enough to be detectable. As we have mentioned before, there are lots of alcohols, and as many acids, which can combine to form a huge number of different esters. The most important, however, are those formed by the action of ethanol on fatty acids, and of higher alcohols on acetic acid. The latter group produce what are known as fruit esters and the flavours of bananas and apples.

Esters are also produced by the action of alcohols on malic, tartaric and lactic acids.

Esters occur in the grapes themselves, and are formed during fermentation and maturation, as acids act on alcohols, in many cases assisted by the action of enzymes. Low fermentation temperatures favour the production of fruity esters and low sulphur dioxide levels and clarification favour ester synthesis and retention in ageing wine. Carbonic maceration and the absence of oxygen during fermentation also favour ester formation. The creation of ethyl acetate is the esterification which has been most studied, since it is the cause of great financial loss when wine goes bad. It is now known that the *Acetobacter* fermentation works by means of a double hit to spoil wine: the bacteria produce ethyl acetate directly; they also produce acetic acid, which, acting on the ethanol in the wine, produces more ethyl acetate.

The fruit esters are typically found in young wines. They fade with age as some of the esters return to their constituent alcohols and acids. The fusel alcohol esters, on the other hand, can pass sensory thresholds with ageing and so become active components of wine flavour.

Not all fruit flavours are due to esters. As already mentioned, ionone is the terpene molecule behind the scent of violets. It is only a hop and a skip chemically speaking from the impressively named 3-(para- hydroxyphenyl)-2-butanone, $C_{10}H_{12}O_2$, which is the compound which gives us the flavour of raspberries.

This molecule is a ketone, a class of compound we shall describe in the section on caramelised aromas. The range of fruit flavours is very large and some are made up of many different compounds. It would be impossible to list them all here, even if their compositions and constituent compounds were known, which in many cases they are not. The blackcurrant flavour, which is so characteristic of wines made from the Cabernet Sauvignon grape, has not been identified. What has been ascertained is that the flavour does *not* arise from the compound which makes blackcurrants taste of blackcurrant.

SPICY AROMAS

We have already touched on the categories of spicy flavour and remarked on the relatively small number of spices cited, and the reasons for the same. There are no subdivisions of this potentially large field of the Aroma Wheel, and the spices quoted are fairly similar in nature. Liquorice and aniseed are grouped together because of the closeness of their chemical as well as their organoleptic nature. Fennel and tarragon could be included in the same group. The active ingredient is anethole, $C_{10}H_{12}O$, a molecule very similar to the terpenes described above.

Eugenol, $C_{10}H_{12}O_2$, differs from anethole only in having one more oxygen atom and a very slight variation in shape. It is a component of oil of cloves, and is in fact an isomer of the raspberry molecule, above.

With pepper we are into a different realm. Piperine, $C_{17}H_{19}O_3N$, is a much more complex molecule, and one which has a nitrogen atom included. It is the active ingredient of both black and white pepper. Piperine is an alkaloid and so related to a number of bitter-tasting substances such as caffeine and quinine. I will spare you the structure, which has two six-member rings and one five-member joined by a branched chain.

It is a little surprising that the list of spicy flavours does not include ginger, which is a familiar enough spice and whose active component, zingerone, $C_{11}H_{14}O_3$, has been identified in some white wines, particularly Riesling.

VEGETATIVE AROMAS

The vegetative group of aromas contains some pretty diverse members. At its core – and the flavours commonly referred to as vegetative – are the bell-pepper, cut-grass, green-bean, straw aromas. The others are relative outsiders. We will look at the former first.

I find that this is the most difficult group of flavours to explain to people. Most folk don't think much about the odour of peppers or grass or asparagus and consequently find difficulty in recognising it. You may recall that in the earlier chapter on wine flavours we remarked on how people will recognise a smell much more readily if they have been confronted by an example or a description, or even a name. It is the unconscious nature of many smells that makes them hard to identify – and few are more unconscious than the grassy section of the vegetative group. Even with training, however, some people find these aromas difficult and some unfortunate folk are unable to recognise them at all.

I have never had a problem of this sort, for I have a very clear mental impression of the smell of new-cut grass. When I was a kid, we lived in a little tenement which had a communal drying green. When the grass grew long, our next-door neighbour would cut it with his scythe (no such affectations as lawnmowers in our part of the town) and pile the grass up into a heap. My friends and I took great delight in jumping off the wall and landing in the pile of grass. I shall never forget the scent of it.

However, not all wine tasters are fortunate enough to have had such a deprived childhood and some method is required for familiarising oneself with vegetative aromas. Ann Noble suggests taking a base wine of little character and immersing a piece of bell pepper in a glass of it. That certainly works. Otherwise, I suggest an acquaintance with as many of the odours mentioned as you can manage and then applying yourself to some wines which are high in vegetative aromas.

There appear to be several sources of vegetative smells. A minor one is the presence of higher alcohols containing six carbons, or hexanols. These compounds occur naturally in some grapes and make the transfer to the wine without losing their character. Higher alcohols are also formed during fermentation, especially if the wine is chaptalised (i.e. has had sugar added to it during fermentation. See the chapter on vinification.). Higher alcohols have very pronounced flavours and one authority claims that these flavours account for 50 per cent of the aromatic constituents of wine, excluding ethanol. It has been suggested that vegetal odours are due to the creation of aldehydes of these hexanols, either in the grapes or at any stage of the wine production, from crushing all the way through to maturation.

Aldehydes are alcohols with hydrogens removed from them, which is what happens when such things are oxidised. The aldehyde with which we are mainly concerned in wine is acetaldehyde, C_2H_4O, which is ethanol lacking two hydrogen atoms. Acetaldehyde is an oxidation product of alcohol, which forms on the way to becoming acetic acid. It is formed in the human liver through the operation of an enzyme, alcohol hydrogenase, and is one of the substances which make us feel so ghastly when we have a hangover.

When detectable, acetaldehyde is generally considered to produce an off-odour. A wine which has been exposed to the air for some time is likely to go off because of the conversion of some of its ethanol to acetaldehyde. That said, acetaldehyde is a major part of the flavour of fino and manzanilla sherries, in which wines it is cultivated as a by-product of the metabolism of the flor yeast. In good sherry the actealdehyde aroma complements the other flavours and is pleasing to a prepared palate. It's an acquired taste, but worth acquiring. There can be few sensations quite so pleasing as eating Spanish omelette and drinking fino sherry straight from the solera, while standing in the cool of a bodega.

The main source of vegetative flavours is undoubtedly the presence of cyclic compounds known as pyrazines. These are like benzene rings, but with two of the carbons replaced by nitrogen atoms, thus:

$$\begin{array}{ccc}
 & N & \\
H-C & & C-H \\
H-C & & C-H \\
 & N &
\end{array}$$

Nitrogen is essential for the growth and metabolism of grapes and yeasts. It is a component of amino acids, upon which all proteins are based. Pyrazines contribute to the flavour of many foods and the splendidly named 2-methoxy-3-isobutylpyrazine has been identified as the main player in the production of the vegetal aroma. It occurs most typically in wines made in cool climates from the Sauvignon Blanc grape, though it is also to be found in those made from Cabernet Sauvignon and Merlot grapes.

The inclusion of eucalyptus and mint in this category is a bit odd, for neither seems to have much in common as regards their smell with the green-grassy aromas. The main mint molecules, menthol and carvone, don't have any nitrogen atoms, though they are both six-carbon cyclical compounds. Carvone is a terpene (see above) and menthol is pretty close.

Tea and tobacco seem to be stretching the category a bit, too. The problem is that the organoleptic categories are imprecise. That's nothing against them: if you follow Wittgenstein's ideas on categories, they are all imprecise at the end of the day. Organoleptic ones are just a bit worse than the others – and that's not surprising, for they are trying to bring together enormous numbers of very different substances under the banner of our subjective sensation.

NUTTY AROMAS

Nutty aromas are mainly to be found in oxidised wines such as sherry. The flor which forms on the surface of fino and manzanilla sherries is produced by the yeast *Saccharomyces cerevisiae*. The yeast oxidises the ethanol in the sherry to acetaldehyde, which is what principally gives sherries their nutty flavour.

The fact that acetaldehyde is present in all wines, if at sub-threshold levels, may explain why nutty aromas are sometimes found: while there is too little acetaldehyde for it to be perceptible on its own, the presence of other flavour substances may bring it to our consciousness.

Besides acetaldehyde, a huge number of other compounds may contribute to nutty flavour in a wine. Most of these are aldehydes or pyrazines – and, as we have seen, it doesn't take much to convert one aldehyde or pyrazine into another, and for the products, together with sub-perceptible acetaldehyde, to bring about a nutty flavour. Diacetyl (see below) is also a component of nutty aromas.

Nutty aromas are sometimes to be found in very old wines, where they are the product of bottle ageing. The active ingredients are likely to be those just mentioned.

CARAMELISED AROMAS

This is not as simple a group as it might seem. The caramel, from which it takes its name, is, as every good cook knows, just burnt sugar. You put some household sugar (sucrose) in a pan with some water, give it heat and, hey presto, you get caramel, which is a lot nicer to eat than the sugar. When sugar is heated, the molecules break up and rearrange themselves. It is the rearrangement which makes the caramel sticky and the break-up products which give it flavour. The simplest of these, acrolein, C_3H_4O, is an aldehyde and slightly acrid-smelling.

That said, though, caramel doesn't smell of much. Completely caramelised sugar doesn't even taste sweet. So while 'caramelised' as a category indicates certain flavour parameters, it doesn't help us much. The main components seem to be sweetness and butter – and appropriately so, since the caramel we eat as a sweet is made using butter as well as sugar. The main source of buttery aromas in wine is

diacetyl, $C_4H_6O_2$, also known as butanedione.

This molecule is one of a group called ketones. Lots of ketones are produced during fermentation, but few of them are discernible except diacetyl. It is a straight-chain propane molecule in which the two middle carbon atoms each has a double-bonded oxygen instead of two hydrogens. Diacetyl has a flavour which has been variously described as being buttery, nutty or toasty – and it is a component of the odour of all three in the originals.

Together with a related ketone, acetoin, diacetyl is to be found in sherries, where, like acetaldehyde, it is tolerated at levels much higher than would be acceptable in an unfortified wine. In the latter case, there is a low threshold, beyond which the flavour imparted by diacetyl becomes a buttery, milky, off-odour.

The scent of vanilla could as well be included under the banner of caramelised aromas, for vanilla is a very common component of caramel-style toffees. Indeed, the correlation is so close that if you ask people to identify vanilla, the most common response is 'toffee'. The inclusion under this heading of honey and butterscotch seems sensible. Both flavours have something in common with that of butter and therefore with diacetyl. Butterscotch, after all, is made by heating together butter, cream and sugar. Honey is a much more varied aroma, in which we find large numbers of rather complex esters.

Molasses, being a partly refined sugar is an obvious inclusion. Chocolate, on the other hand, is less self-evidently a member of the group – especially the very dark, bitter chocolates, which must be at the very edge of the category, along with soy sauce. Most chocolate has vanillin in its recipe, however, which may account for its organoleptic similarity to butterscotch, even if it contains very little sugar. And it has fats, which give it a pleasant, buttery mouth-feel.

WOODY AROMAS

When we get to woody aromas, we begin to move into the territory of the nasty, for some of the scents listed are not such as would be welcomed in the flavour of a wine. Vanilla is OK, for it is rarely that one would wish it absent. As a spice, it is extracted from the seed pods of an orchid grown in the tropics. Its formula is $C_8H_8O_3$ and its structure remarkably similar to many of the flavour compounds we have already inspected.

Vanilla in wine is mainly the result of oak cooperage. It is produced by the decomposition of the long-chain lignin molecules which are wood's principal component. These molecules are, as remarked before, polymerised glucose units which, once separated from each other, do not require a great leap to form a vanillin molecule.

Vanilla is unusual among flavour components in that, though it has a very low detection threshold, its intensity very quickly peaks, so that no matter how much more vanillin is present, we do not register it as tasting stronger. As a result, you can't get too much vanilla: a property virtually unique among wine flavonoids.

Given the source of vanillin, it isn't too surprising that it should be grouped as a woody flavour alongside oak – for the oaky flavours in wine mostly derive from the components of the oak casks which contain it or – in some cases – from oak chips which are soaked in the wine so as to impart an oaky flavour. But there the congruence ends, for the flavour of oak is due to tannins, whose aroma is very different from that of vanillin. Admittedly, the wine is going to pick up vanillin along with the tannins, and the latter greatly improves the taste of the former, but even so, the two flavours don't resemble each other in the slightest. It would seem that here the Aroma Wheel is sacrificing organoleptic consistency to categorial convenience.

The cork can be a source of woody odours. In old wines, the cork has been in contact with the wine for a very long time and there is likely to be an extraction of aromatics from it. If we reflect that the cork oak is a member of the genus *Quercus* just as are the oaks used to make the barrel staves, this isn't too surprising.

Phenolic and resinous flavours can arise in the course of fermentation and maturation. They are probably desirable if at very low levels, but beyond a low threshold they become off-odours – unless, that is, you have a taste for resinous wines of the sort produced in Greece and Cyprus. These wines are flavoured by the pine resin, which is introduced in the course of fermentation. Originally used with a view to preserving wines in a hot climate, resin has become a traditional flavouring and is recognised as such by the EU. It has little to recommend it in terms of the flavours normally regarded as desirable in wine. But, like a lot of worse things, you can get to like it, given time. At least you don't have to worry about minute traces of woody or phenolic flavours.

EARTHY AROMAS

The best known of the earthy-mouldy group of off-odours is that of mouldy cork. This is the aroma you are mostly looking for when the wine waiter gives you a sample to nose. You may not have met it yet, but when you do, you will be in no doubt. It is caused by a chlorine compound called 2,4,6-tricholoroanisole, normally referred to as 2,4,6-TCA. This is a benzene ring with three chlorine atoms attached.

It arises because chlorine-containing fungicides are used on the cork trees, or because chlorine is used to bleach cork stoppers. It has a distinctive musty, mouldy aroma and is detectable at very low thresholds indeed. Its threshold, curiously, is raised with increasing alcoholic strength, so that, though it is often present in distilled wine products, it is rarely discernible.

There are various other causes of mouldy taint in wines: the growth of some bacteria, such as *Streptomyces*; the presence of various fungi, and, surprisingly, cask oakwood. Some of the mouldy odours have been sourced to a rather complicated molecule, 2-methoxy-3-isoproplypyrazine. This, and others, can cause a greater or lesser degree of mustiness and mouldiness – but none are as powerful as 2,4,6-TCA.

CHEMICAL AROMAS

There is a variant on the Anna Karenina principle at work in wines. You will no doubt recall the opening lines of Tolstoy's novel: 'Happy families are all alike: every unhappy family is unhappy in its own way.' While it isn't true to say that all good wines are alike, they do conform to certain norms. Bad wines, on the other hand, can be bad in all sorts of different ways, each of which is caused by one or more of a rich and varied lot of substances. The list of chemical off-odours makes this clear. There are a great many evil flavour components, any one of which is capable of rendering a wine undrinkable.

Of the chemical off-notes, by far the greatest number have organo-sulphur compounds of some sort as their active ingredient. This is our first encounter with sulphur in this essay. A chemical element, it is one of the commonest elements in the earth's crust and is present in the atmosphere as sulphur dioxide, SO_2, and sulphuric acid, H_2SO_4 – in which latter form it is a major component of acid rain. Sulphur is deeply involved in wine in several ways. The proteins and amino acids in the grapes contain sulphur atoms, elemental sulphur dust is used as a fungicide in the vineyard, and sulphur dioxide is widely used in wine making to prevent oxidation of must and wine, and to suppress the growth of wild yeasts and bacteria. It is not too surprising, therefore, that sulphur crops up in the finished wine, in all sorts of combinations, most of them undesirable, and some calamitous.

The simplest form of sulphur contaminant is hydrogen sulphide, H_2S, being a sulphur atom with two attached hydrogens. Hydrogen sulphide gives us the smell of rotten eggs and is perennially popular among juveniles as stink bombs. At low levels, that is: in fact hydrogen sulphide is as toxic as hydrogen cyanide and at high concentrations will kill you stone dead in an instant. What is more, at toxic levels, you don't get the warning of the bad smell, for it seems we don't detect it if it is going to kill us. Of course, it may be just that nobody has survived to tell us.

Hydrogen sulphide contamination in wine can arise from the degradation of amino acids in the grape tissue, from sulphates also found in the grape tissue, from sulphur dioxide, and from elemental sulphur dusting of the vines. Traces of H_2S are to be found in all wines, but usually below sensory thresholds – which means at very low levels indeed, for we can detect the compound at concentrations as low as a few parts per trillion. At sub-threshold level, hydrogen sulphide adds to the complexity and interest of a wine; above the threshold, is renders it quite foul and usually undrinkable.

Since it has no carbon atoms, hydrogen sulphide is classed as an inorganic compound. Sulphur does, however, enter into a great many organic molecules, which are known as organo-sulphur compounds. The great majority of organo-sulphur compounds found in wine are extremely unpleasant and wine makers go to great lengths to prevent their formation or, if formed, to remove them. Mercaptans or, as they are now more usually called, thiols, are the most troublesome of the organo-sulphurs, for they are produced both in vinification and in maturation, are difficult to remove during vinification, and by the time their formation in maturation is discovered, it's usually too late.

The Aroma Wheel lists mercaptan as one of the off-odours, and also skunk, whose fine aroma is also due to the scent of a mercaptan. For connoisseurs of esoteric wine off-notes, a trip to the eastern USA is a must. As we noted in the first chapter, it is quite impossible to describe the smell of skunk, for there is nothing with which one can compare it – but once smelt, never forgotten. Even the merest whiff of long-gone skunk is deeply upsetting: being sprayed by a skunk is, I suspect, an experience from which one's olfactory memory would never recover. The active component of skunk perfume is an organo-sulphur called 3-methylbutane-1-thiol, $C_5H_{12}S$.

It just shows what three simple sorts of atom are capable of: that a few carbons and hydrogens and one measly sulphur should be able to cause us such grief, is quite astonishing. At least it's astonishing to me. No doubt it's not astonishing to the skunk, but it is certainly useful to it. It is a little surprising that humans have never sought to emulate the skunk and use scent in warfare. An army which was breathing in 3-methylbutane-1-tiol would be rendered completely helpless, but would be otherwise unharmed. Maybe the problem – apart from conventions on chemical weapons – is that if the wind turned, the victors could find themselves hoist by their own petard.

The other scents listed under sulphur in the Aroma Wheel are all caused by organo-sulphur compounds (except hydrogen sulphide and sulphur dioxide) but the mercaptans are by far the most potent when it comes to spoiling wine. Rotten cabbage – never a flavour you want in your wine – is caused by methyl mercaptan, and what is politely called a barnyard odour (for which read shit) is down to 2-mercaptoethanol.

The off-notes classed under petroleum have various origins, some of which are known, some (such as tar, surprisingly) not. While disagreeable, their incidence is not as common as that of the sulphur compounds, nor is their presence as calamitous. Kerosene aromas can be created when aromatic hydrocarbons break down and the smell of plastic is usually down to styrene, a cyclic hydrocarbon occasionally found in wine. Papery off-notes originate in the use of unsuitable filter materials.

Pungency is more a matter of nasal sensation than of smell proper. All the compounds listed, if present in sufficiently high concentrations, will cause the tissues of the nasal sinus to register sensations akin to those of pain. The exact mechanism for this is not known, but it is thought that pungent aromas stimulate the endings of the trigeminal nerve, the nerve through which we feel pain in the tissues of the face.

The off-odours grouped under 'Other' are a mixed lot. Fusel alcohols have been mentioned above: these are the higher alcohols which at low levels contribute to complexity but at anything much above threshold, are disagreeable. They are the result of yeast metabolism during fermentation. Sorbate is the rancid-butter odour which comes from an excess of potassium sorbate, a fungicide which is widely used in the food and drink industry. When sorbates are used in wine, lactic acid bacteria can metabolise the sorbates to produce high levels of the odour of geranium leaves, which are disagreeable to most palates. Fishy and soapy flavours are usually the result of the metabolism of various bacteria.

PUNGENT AROMAS

Alcohol causes a sensation of heat and menthol of coolness. This is because alcohol and menthol stimulate respectively the hot and cold temperature receptors on the skin. When alcohol is present, the temperature sensors are affected and register the sensation as that of heat. Similarly, when menthol forms the environment of the nerve ending, the nerve fires at temperatures far above those at which it normally functions, causing us to have a sensation of coolness. Menthol, $C_{10}H_{20}O$, is a cyclic compound with an –OH ending, which is not dissimilar to many of the molecules we have examined. It is produced in small quantities during fermentation.

OXIDISED AROMAS

The effect of oxidation at various stages in the production and maturation of wine is discussed above. The oxidation with which we are concerned here is the production of acetaldehyde as a result of oxidation in bottle. (The intentional oxidation in cask in the production of sherry is not considered an off-odour and is not our concern here.) Oxidation happens when the cork is faulty and air is allowed access to the wine in bottle. There are various reasons for this. If the bottle is stored for long periods in a vertical position, the cork will dry out and shrink, so that it no longer effectively seals the wine from the air. Rapid changes of temperature can have the same effect, as can the use of faulty corks, or corks which are not properly inserted.

When the wine oxidises, acetaldehyde is produced at levels sufficient for it to cause a flat off-odour. As levels rise, the aroma becomes strangely chemical and difficult to describe, like bad sherry. The wine changes colour: red wines become brown and then yellow; white wines become yellow.

MICROBIOLOGICAL AROMAS

This is a field almost as big as wine itself, so many are the possible ways in which the actions of microorganisms can affect the flavour of wines. The principal agents, however, are relatively few. Wine is made using the wild yeasts which occur on the skins of the grape, or cultured yeasts which are introduced in their place. Yeasts are micro-cellular organisms which are neither quite plant nor animal, but have some of the characteristics of both. There are lots of different kinds of yeast, and besides their function in converting the sugars of the grape into alcohol, yeasts have a flavour. (More: many yeasts have very strong flavours and are widely used in the food industry for flavouring all sorts of savoury products. When you eat smoky barbecue-flavour crisps, the flavour comes from yeasts.) If any yeast is left in the wine, it is likely to make its presence known in the flavour. Most wines are filtered to remove yeasts and any other solids. However, especially in the case of very fine red wines, the wine may be unfiltered and the dead yeast settle as part of the sediment. If the sediment is allowed into the wine in the glass, it will taste yeasty.

The lactic acid bacteria responsible for the malolactic secondary fermentation in red wines can, if the wine is stored in warm conditions, produce spoilage. This takes various forms, described as sauerkraut-like or mousy. Mousiness is associated with certain strains of *Lactobacillus*, which in the course of their metabolism synthesise complex nitrogen compounds known as hydropyridines. Butyric acid is another of the typical products of lactic bacteria. It smells disgusting.

FLAVOUR ORIGINS
≈THE GRAPE≈

The first and most important source of flavour in wine is the grape. It is an old and persuasive saying, that you can make bad wine from good grapes, but you can't make good wine from bad grapes. This is because the wine maker, like any other artisan, must apply his skill to the materials in hand. If the material is good, and if he has the ability and the patience, then the finished product will be a good one – be he (or she) a cook or a smith or a turner or a toolmaker or a cabinetmaker or a boatbuilder or the maker of any of the great number of things which are, even today, the product of hand and eye rather than machine. A skilled workman or woman can make a passable product from inferior materials, but never an excellent one. The same is true of wines. From indifferent grapes, the skilled wine maker can, by the application of skill and knowledge, produce a drinkable wine with no obvious faults. But he or she can never make a good wine from such stuff, let alone a great one. The reason, as we have seen, is that goodness in wine, once the requisites of sweetness, acidity and tannins have been satisfied, depends on a host of flavour components which either were themselves present in the grapes, or are created from stuff which was.

As we learnt in the chapter on wine flavours, the science of classification is called taxonomy. Its heyday was the 19th century, when gentlemen swanned around the globe, collecting as many different sorts of creatures as possible. When they got home, the gentlemen would arrange the creatures and write papers about them. If the critters hadn't been discovered by anyone else, the gentlemen got to name them. The names were all in Latin, to show other gentlemen that the scientific gentlemen weren't ignorant peasants and to show the peasants that the scientific gentlemen really were gentlemen, despite their ungentlemanly habit of digging around in the dirt and suchlike activities. The critters (which term includes plants) were allocated to genus or species, according to their morphological characteristics – which is a fancy way of saying that they were arranged so that things which looked more or less alike were classed as being in the same family. What got put in which category often depended on who was doing the putting, which caused a fair amount of confusion. As a method, it isn't impressively scientific, but it's the best one can do, and things get rearranged from time to time and by and by we get a pretty reliable sort of classification of everything alive, or at least of those which we know about. Modern methods of DNA analysis are an improvement, but involve essentially the same method, only with rather classier tools.

One of the great problems with biological classification is that living things have a tendency to change; old types disappear and new ones emerge, as plants or animals evolve in response to changing environments. What drives this process is the tendency – which all living things exhibit – to throw up sports, or genetic mutations. Darwin's great contribution was to show how, on the basis of random mutation and the survival advantage which might accrue from mutation, species could evolve to occupy vacant environmental niches and to supplant less-evolved species in existing habitats.

There can be no doubt at all as to who are the winners in this game. Beetles leave the rest of us standing: indeed, they leave us all miles behind, for there are more different species of beetle than there are other species put together. There are some respectable runners-up, though, among which the genus *Vitis* in the family *Vitaceae* gets an honourable mention. The *Vitaceae* are climbing plants whose seeds are enclosed in berries. They all have leaves which stick out on alternate sides of the shoots, with flowers or tendrils developing opposite each leaf. The *Vitaceae* family has a little over a thousand known members, mostly living in tropical or sub-tropical environments. Virginia creeper is a member of the family, as are various ivies and all sorts of vines. The family is divided into fifteen or sixteen sub-families, or genuses, depending on which taxonomical opinion you favour.

The genus with which we are concerned is *Vitis*, the grapevine. Its member species have a very high mutation rate, which has enabled it to occupy environmental slots in Europe, Asia and the Americas. Fossil remains of *Vitis* have been found which show that it has been around for at least fifty-five million years. About ten thousand years ago, at the end of the last glaciation, various species of *Vitis* evolved in Eurasia, the Americas and in China. The latter two regions, probably because of the north–south orientation of their mountain ranges, evolved numerous species of *Vitis*: China around thirty species and Northern and Central America about thirty-four. Europe, on the same hypothesis (i.e. because its mountain barriers run east–west), evolved only one species: *Vitis vinifera*. It was the Eurasians' good fortune that this species is the one from which you can make decent wine.

Vitis vinifera (literally, in Latin: the wine-bearing vine), is the vine which bears the grapes from which we make the wine. It makes its first appearance to palaeobotany about ten thousand years ago, in southern France, at the end of the last Ice Age. The first signs of domestication are found in the Fertile Crescent of northeast modern Iran and southern Anatolia around six thousand years ago. From then on, it appears to have spread quite rapidly: there is reason to think that, by 2700 BC, the species was domesticated in England, as well as in many places between there and Mesopotamia (southwest Asia). The story of the spread of the cultivars of the grapevine, *Vitis vinifera*, has often been told: how it travelled in ancient times into Israel and Egypt; then into Greece; how the Greeks took it wherever they settled, in Italy, France and Spain; how the Romans took it to Germany and England. From the Greeks onward, there are pictorial and written historical sources to support the abundant archaeological record.

It would seem, therefore, that we can just accept the account and leave it at that: folk somewhere in the Middle East found out how to use the mutability of *Vitis vinifera* to produce decent grapes for eating and wine making, and then the knowledge spread out along whatever routes people travelled. I have two problems with this account. Neither of them will cause us to enjoy our wine the less, but if, as I hope, we accept that understanding is necessary for appreciation, they should be aired.

The first problem is that this account does not square with the palaeobotanical record, which clearly shows that *Vitis vinifera* variants – and presumably cultivars – existed long before the Greeks began their voyaging. There is no dispute about the transfer from Mesopotamia into Israel or Egypt (where there appear to have been no indigenous vines), but there is evidence (from seed and pollen shape) of domesticated grapevines which long preceded the westward dispersal of the great agricultural revolution of 3000–2000 BC and certainly antedated the commercial activities of Mycenean Greece, let alone those of classical times. Since human beings had settled those regions long before the historical period, it seems probable that the domestication of *Vitis vinifera* arose independently in many places. (Studies in the history of science in the last 30 years have shown that there is a tendency for people in different places, who have no connection with each other, to devise the same hypotheses at the same time. Since today's scientists are no smarter than their ancestors were five thousand years ago – evolution of intelligence being a very slow affair – there is no reason why the same thing should not have happened in early agriculture.)

There is some evidence that people began to make wine almost as soon as they had developed decent grapes. In virtually all Indo-European languages, the words for 'wine' and 'vine' have the same root, while the terms for 'grape' have for the most part different roots.

The second problem with the account of the dispersal of the grapevine is and is not a serious one. It isn't that there is doubt about whether the account is true: the question is, whose truth is it? You may recall that we mentioned in the opening chapter the traditional Victorian picture of evolution, with protozoans at the bottom and Man at the top. You may also recall that this image has been largely discarded, as being a distortion whose object is to put Man at the top of the tree. The account of the spread of the grapevine is similarly anthropocentric: it is an account of the matter from a purely human point of view. If we look at things from the angle of the grapevine, they take on a different aspect, in which humans, from being the masters of the universe, become simply one more ecological opportunity. The development of the technology of travel, whether wheeled vehicles or ships with sails – or jet aircraft, for that matter – becomes, from this point of view, just another set of vectors, on a par with birds' bellies or beasts' furs.

Now all this may seem a bit academic, but it's not. Consider: the vine mutates, the successful mutations succeed and the unsuccessful fail. One of the successful mutations is the development of seed berries which birds and beasts find desirable as food, for those birds and beasts disperse the seeds. Humans try the berries and like them. Humans, being smart, work out that some berries taste better than others and cultivate the better vines. *Vitis vinifera* achieves its huge success by its ability to produce grapes which are tailored to the gustatory apparatus of human beings – an apparatus which evolved quite independently of the grapevine. Hence the nice taste of grapes. Hence also our liking for the wines made from those grapes. It isn't an accident after all.

As a strategy for survival, it is hard to beat. And subtle, too. For the same evolutionary device which allows grapes to grow in rich soils and produce luscious fruit for eating, also allows a mutant of the species to adapt to poor soils and, in some cases, marginal climates. In such environments the mutant produces smaller, less-rich berries, and fewer of them, but because of the flavours contributed by the micronutrients which deep roots extract from poor soils, the berries contain the flavour precursors which will make great wines, and the mutant appeals to human taste on quite another level. I'm tempted to say, cunning – but of course that would imply teleology, and we can't have that in a discussion of evolutionary change, for Laplace got it wrong.

So, you may be asking, what has all this to do with flavour? What it means is this: natural selection has tailored grapes (and thus wines) so that they have a chemical affinity with our gustatory apparatus and therefore taste nice. We are now going to look at the results of a few millennia of selective adaptation. We will do so with the intention of remarking on what it is about the different sorts of grapes which make the wines made from them taste nice.

We should perhaps enter a caveat here: I said earlier that you mustn't expect too much. The identification of the flavours of grape varietals is a science in its infancy, or at least delayed adolescence. As far as can presently be ascertained, most grape varieties do not produce distinctive flavours. A few do, but only in rare cases has the impact compound been isolated. So if you find yourself at a wine tasting, and some prat starts going on about the balance of the Merlot and Mourvèdre in the blend, you can know for sure that it's just wind: except in rare cases, there is nobody who can tell, from the aromas alone, what grapes have been used to make a particular wine. The exceptions are wines made from varieties other than *Vitis vinifera*, such as the *Vitis labrusca* of North America (which is pretty nasty), and highly distinctive *vinifera* varietals such as Gewürztraminer and Muscat. Even in the case of the last two, you have to know your stuff to be sure that the Gewürztraminer isn't a particularly flowery Riesling or maybe an unusually acidic Muller Thurgau, and to distinguish the Muscat from a spicy Sauternes. We shall begin with the white wines, for the exercise is marginally easier in their case, mainly because most white wines are drunk young, and ageing complicates an already complicated situation.

In what follows, we shall consider only a few of the so-called 'classic' grape varieties. The number of *vinifera* cultivars is unknown, but is certainly large. In practice, most wines which the average drinker is likely to taste are made from a relatively small number of varietals. Since, as we have said above, the problem of attributing flavours even to those is a knotty one, there is no point in complicating things by talking of obscure grape types. There are plenty of books which will tell you more than you are likely to need to know about such things, especially in view of the fact that most of those grapes do not produce distinctively flavoured wines – or at least wines whose flavour anyone can reliably attribute to the grape variety.

CHARDONNAY

It is perhaps as well that the proprietors of established classic French wines continue to use only the name of the vineyard and the year as means of identifying the wine. Those drinkers who have acquired a taste for the big, oaky Chardonnays of Australia and California would find the white wines of Burgundy rather surprising, for there is little in the flavour to indicate that the wines are all made from the same grape varietal, Chardonnay. It is said that most New World wine makers setting out to plant Chardonnay vines do so with the example of Burgundy uppermost in their minds. If that is the case, then some of them fall far short of their ambitions. For between the supermarket bottle of cheap, heavily oaked Californian or Aussie Chardonnay and the wines of Montrachet or Meursault there is little apparent congruence as regards flavour. Maybe I'm being unfair in making such a comparison, though, without mentioning the great Chardonnays from northern Sonoma or Napa, which are good enough to challenge the Burgundy classics on their own territory, or the Australian Chardonnay wines which show real character.

Chardonnay is attractive to wine makers, and the possibility of producing a flinty Chablis or a steely Montrachet is no doubt a worthy ambition. But the aspirations of most folk who plant new Chardonnay vines are more likely to be influenced by the ease with which Chardonnay can be grown, its tolerance of large variations in climate, its early ripening, its high sugars and its good yield. After all, a decently made Chardonnay will find a market almost anywhere, and secure a return on effort and capital, even though nobody would mistake it for a Grand Cru Burgundy.

In evolutionary terms, Chardonnay is a very ancient cultivar. It is said that its origins in the Fertile Crescent are evidenced by its long-established presence in Syria and Lebanon, which, despite the disapproval of Islam, are two of the oldest wine-making locations. Whatever its origins, its virtues have clearly long been recognised by viticulturists and wine makers. Treated properly, it will make wines in a great variety of styles, all of them seemingly appropriate to the grape, for the grape shows a quite astonishing capacity to exhibit flavour. Lots of different flavours, that is, though not any single flavour or collection of flavours by which its wine can be definitely characterised.

Different regions produce strikingly different Chardonnay-based wines. Acidity and sweetness depend on growing conditions, on harvesting and on the many variations of vinification technique. But within regions where such differences are at a minimum, the variation in flavour is remarkable, and one vineyard's Chardonnay wine will be fruity, while another's positively savoury. Corton-Charlemagne will be nutty while Meursault is buttery; Montrachet will show fruit over steel, while the next vineyard's wine tastes of honey. Vineyards a short distance away still will produce wines which taste of melon, while others could be mistaken, in their green-grassy flavour, for a Sauvignon Blanc. It is common for a Chablis to be described as smelling of apples and for the very best to have just a hint of shit.

Most of the Chardonnay wines on analysis are shown to contain B-damascenone, a ketone with an intense, rose-like, scent, which contributes to the flowery component of their make-up. But apart from that, chemists have so far failed to identify uniquely characteristic aroma compounds. Certainly, some Chardonnays show aromatic flavours which are similar to those found in oak wood, so that the practice of fermenting and maturing in oak can be seen as an enhancement of natural flavours rather than simply as an extraneous coloration. How far it is permissible to go down this road is a matter for the opinion of the individual wine maker and, eventually, for the market. The hint of shit is probably due to sulphur compounds produced during vinification.

The variety of aromas of which Chardonnay wines are capable gives comfort to the supporters of *terroir* as the determinant of flavour. That is, if the same grape is made into wine by traditional methods which do not vary significantly, then striking variations in flavour between vineyards would appear to be the consequence of variation in the micronutrients the vine draws from the soil. Even if we allow for the influence of different microclimates within a small region, and variations in harvesting, vinification and maturation, we still find that there are inexplicable differences of flavour. It does not seem too far-fetched to attribute these to those minute variations in circumstance collectively referred to as *terroir*.

Chardonnay grapes are being grown today in almost every wine-making region of the world. The styles and flavours of the wines vary greatly, the great majority of them being consumed while young, so the flavour variations which come with age in bottle are not commonly a matter for concern. Chardonnay is not a wine which, even at its best, takes well to long ageing, though if the initial acidity is high it will improve in bottle for ten or twenty years. Then the tannins, which are present even in un-oaked wines, will soften and the flavours mellow as the colour darkens.

RIESLING

Riesling is one of the few grapes in which distinctive flavour components have been identified. Wines made from Riesling grapes are distinctive and often distinguished. Riesling is the cold-climate grape *par excellence*, the vine flourishing in its native Germany at latitudes and altitudes at which no other wine-making grape of quality will ripen. The vine is indigenous to Germany. It is thought to be a domesticated variety of *Vitis vinifera sylvestris*, a wild vine which grows in the Rhineland. It is identifiable in 15th-century records, and some historians identify it with a vine described by Pliny in the 1st century AD. It is unquestionably the finest German vine, and some respected authorities (not necessarily German) reckon Riesling wines to be the finest white wines made anywhere.

In Germany, Riesling wines are made as far north as the Rheingau and Mosel, in which regions they are late-ripening, the berries rarely being picked before October and, for the sweetest wines, as late as January. The uniquely German method of determining ripeness by selective picking of bunches and even berries allows control of the level of sugars in the wine – if at the risk of the weather turning bad and aborting the harvest. The long growing period and late harvesting mean that wines may have high levels of both sweetness and sugars and the Beerenauslesen and Trockenbeerenauslesen wines are quite extraordinary, like slightly alcoholic fruit cordials.

While its characteristic expression is to be found in Germany, Riesling is planted in various places throughout the rest of Europe (though not in France, where the appellation laws confine it to a small part of Alsace), in the USA, Canada and Australasia. The soils and conditions in which it is grown vary greatly from those of Germany, as do the climates, for Riesling will tolerate less-cool climates, with a change of character, but without losing quality. It is not nearly so fashionable a wine as Chardonnay, and the acreage planted is a small fraction of that of Chardonnay, despite the ability of Riesling grapes to produce elegant, refined and toothsome wines in a large variety of styles, from bone-dry to extremely sweet – and all of them with a distinctive Riesling flavour.

So in what does that flavour consist? Unusually, we have a handle on the flavour, in the form of monoterpene alcohols, which are found in Muscat and Riesling wines. Terpenes, you will recall, are compounds based on the five-carbon isoprene rubber ring. Monoterpene alcohols are isoprene units with -OH endings which are characteristic of alcohols. The levels of these compounds in Rieslings are lower than in Muscats, which is why Riesling is the classier wine of the two for, as we have seen, in-your-face flavours are rarely those which create the overall impression of quality. The monoterpene alcohols are responsible for some of the flowery-spicy aromas of Riesling wines. The honey flavour is another matter. Some of it may be due to traces of diacetyl, for butter along with sweetness is commonly perceived as honey. Otherwise, it's anybody's guess. Having said that, which is about all we can say with any assurance as regards the sources of Riesling varietal flavours, we are left again with a feeling that organic chemistry, for all its successes in other fields, has as yet come nowhere near to explaining just why the finest wines taste as they do.

SAUVIGNON BLANC

I remember many years ago saying to my friend Zubair, who is a paragon among wine merchants, that Sancerres were not much to my taste, being, as I thought, too acid and rather lacking in character. Zubair rose to the challenge, said tactfully that I was dead wrong, and proceeded to lead me through a series of wines, first Sancerres and then, for it seemed like a good idea, some other expressions of the Sauvignon Blanc grape. I soon got the idea. Certainly, the stuff can be tart, flat and uninteresting. It can also be perfectly brilliant: lots of fruity flavours on top of green grass, and enough acidity to balance the fruit but not sufficient to make the wine seem sour. It was a memorable experience and one I recommend to those who don't know Zubair.

A few months later, I managed to wangle some tickets for the London Wine Fair. With a couple of my chums, I set out to see what there was, tasting my way systematically through the many expressions of each grape variety. The Sauvignon Blancs were as I had by then come to expect, and very pleasing, and it was hard to say which we liked the best. Until, that is, we came to the Cloudy Bay. History makes it unnecessary to describe our reaction: enough to say that that was the year the world sat up and took notice of this hitherto unremarked New Zealand wine. My sister, I'm pleased to say, had the sense to buy several cases at what was later seen to be a very advantageous price.

The fashion for wines made from the Sauvignon Blanc grape is a modern phenomenon. The grape has long been important, but in combination with Semillon, in blends which make the great white wines of Sauternes and Graves. As a single-grape wine, Sauvignon Blanc is a recent addition to the wine lists of Britain and America compared with veterans such as Chardonnay and Riesling. The attraction of the wine is in accord with a larger fashion in white wines: for clean, crisp, fruity, young wines. In fact the grape has been grown for centuries around Bordeaux, the Loire and in other parts of France. Its translation to other parts of Europe, North and South America, Australia and New Zealand is a matter of the last few decades. The main force behind its expansion has been Robert Mondavi who, making wine from Californian grapes, moderated their grassiness by maturation in oak and sold the resulting potation to American customers as Fumé Blanc, an authentically American product whose French name added a cosmopolitan feel to the comfort provided by its domestic provenance. The power of the enormous US market was sufficient to create interest among wine makers elsewhere and to encourage experimentation with the grape, which has had two happy consequences: very fine Sauvignon Blanc wines have been made in several parts of the world, and the original, French expressions of the grape have found new markets.

The attraction of Sauvignon Blanc wines is not difficult to understand. At their worst, they are merely sharp and acid, but rarely offensive. At best, though the acidity is often enough to set the teeth on edge, it is balanced by great fruit underlaid by just enough of the green-grass flavour to make for a very satisfying drink. A drink, what is more, for a sunny restaurant or the open air, not the musty salons and dining rooms of days gone by. It is a wine for modern times.

The source of the acidity is no great mystery; that of the fruitiness less clear, for the fruits we have here are unusual ones: gooseberries, mostly – other fruits are rarely mentioned, save occasionally lychees, passion and citrus fruits. We can put names to a few of the impact compounds in this case: mostly thiols or mercaptans – foul-smelling compounds which above threshold are most displeasing, but below it, and in combination with other aromas, can be agreeable. But by far the most distinctive flavour which characterises Sauvignon Blanc wines is the green-grassy–bell-pepper group of aromas described in the chapter on wine flavours. So well-established is the relationship, that the description is often put the other way round, and students trying to grasp that particular aroma are asked to think of Sauvignon Blanc.

This group of flavours is, as we have remarked, due mainly to the presence of 2-methoxy-3-isobutylpyrazine – helped out by its close cousins, iso-propyl and sec-butyl pyrazines, which are to be found in Sauvignon Blanc wines, if at rather lower levels than the main player. These compounds are probably implicated in the gooseberry flavour, along with esters of the various acids and alcohols. Their aromas must be kept at a low level if the wine is not to be overwhelmed. If it is, the more complimentary descriptions become pejorative and the phrase 'cat's piss' is sometimes heard. This imbalance is commonly produced when the vine's vegetative growth is excessive. It can be curbed by rigorous pruning and the use of rootstocks which are less productive.

The aroma of some Sauvignon Blanc wines, especially of some Pouilly-Fume and Sancerre, is sometimes described as 'flinty'. Now this appellation is something of a mystery, for flint doesn't have a smell. It seems that the description derives from an older term, 'gunflint', which is more comprehensible, as referring to the odour created when the flint of a flintlock gun strikes the pan. That does have a smell: a funky, sulphurous odour created when the flint sparks. The odour may derive to some extent from the sparking flint, but a much more likely source is to be found in the proximity of gunpowder. For a flintlock gun is fired when the sparks from the flint striking the steel of the frison fly into the pan and ignite the gunpowder which the latter contains. Old-fashioned gunpowder consists of carbon, nitre and sulphur, and when it goes off it leaves a cloud of dense black smoke and a heavy smell of sulphur. Years after the gun has been fired, the smell of sulphur clings to its parts, so it is not too surprising that flint should be thought to have a sulphurous odour. That very good Sauvignon Blanc wines do so smell, is not in doubt: a Loire correlate of the faecal smell of great Burgundy.

The effect of age on Sauvignon Blanc wines is curious. In blended form, in Sauternes, it can last for a long time without changing: neither improving nor deteriorating. I have read, in works by respectable writers, that it can last a hundred years without alteration. I think a touch of scepticism is in order here: how does anyone know what a wine was like a century ago? We don't know what it was like when it went into the bottle, so how can we make a comparison? We can read descriptions of Sauternes a century ago, possibly even descriptions of Sauternes newly bottled, but, knowing how poorly even the best descriptions can approximate to the flavour of a wine, we may be permitted a pinch of salt.

What we can know is that Sauvignon Blanc is the partner of a marriage made in vinous heaven, to Semillon, whose blessed progeny are the sweet wines of Sauternes and Graves. The acidity and zest of the Sauvignon Blanc added to the lusciousness of the Semillon, produce wines that balance sweetness with tartness, body with wings.

SEMILLON

Semillon follows naturally from any discussion of Sauvignon Blanc, in virtue of their famous partnership in Bordeaux. The vine is planted widely throughout the world, and is valued for its docility and its ability to produce wines which have low acidity and plenty of alcohol, and are lacking in any distinctive character. Even in France, which has much larger plantings of Semillon than anywhere else, few wine makers show any interest in making fine wines from Semillon grapes unblended. In its homeland, it is a workhorse, valued only for what can be loaded on its back. With one exception: when it is infected by the noble rot (*Botrytis cinerea*). Then the rot concentrates and complicates the flavour components, raises sugar levels to otherwise impossible heights, but nevertheless maintains and even augments acidity. That is when Semillon comes into its own. Even then, though, it is usually blended with Sauvignon Blanc.

The grape is planted widely in Chile, as part of that country's love affair with classic Bordeaux grapes. The variety grows extremely well there, the vines setting large, pale-green, thin-skinned grapes. Alas, though unblended wines are made from the grape in Chile, the results are not such as to encourage the experiment, lacking, as they do, the acidity necessary for a properly palatable wine. This is generally the curse of Semillon.

It would appear that the answer, as with Riesling and Chardonnay, must be to plant in cooler climates, in the hope that acidity will rise without prejudice to whatever fruit flavours the grape may contain. Alas, for Semillon, the only consequence of a cooler environment is likely to be the development of vegetative flavours similar to those of Sauvignon Blanc, at levels prejudicial to enjoyment, without any quid pro quo as regards other flavours. Things are little better in most places where the varietal is grown: in Argentina and South Africa, most of Australasia, and parts of eastern Europe. Little Semillon is grown in the USA.

All this might be enough to make you wonder why the variety is included in any book about the flavour of wines. The justification is to be found in one place on the planet: Hunter Valley, New South Wales, Australia. There, Semillon wines are made which are the wonder of the vinous world. They are dry, white and gorgeous: greenish and lemony when young, with age they mature to show buttery, toasty flavours which would not disgrace a great wine anywhere in the world. It is difficult to know what conclusion to draw from this, and one falls back on the notion of *terroir*. The Hunter Valley must possess a microclimate and geology which, combined, provide the micronutrients that, when concentrated by Semillon's unique chemistry, produce the flavours of a great wine.

CHENIN BLANC

It is a curious thing that so many of the historical records of European vines seem to begin in the 15th century. Curious, that is, until you remember what things were like before then: the Black Death, the Hundred Years' War, and so on. Life may not have been a bed of roses in the 15th century and thereafter, but things were never quite so bad, or calamity quite so universal, again. Agriculture recovered, production surpluses appeared, and what was left of the population was able to start again to make some decent wine. At Mont-Chenin on a tributary of the Loire, the monks cultivated a white grape and made wine from it. The wine was sharp, but tasty, and went very well with pig-fat and such-like delicacies. It did then and it does today. Charcuterie is one of the joys of French country life, and there is no better accompaniment for *rillettes* or *andouillettes* than a crisp Chenin Blanc, as it is made in the Loire.

Anyone who has drunk the wines of Anjou or Touraine knows what acidity is: these are wines for drinking with food – and preferably fatty food at that, for the acidity is sometimes so high that, taken on their own, the drier wines of Vouvray or Saumur can make for uncomfortable drinking. Happily, tartness is not the end of the matter, otherwise there would be little for us to say about the grape, and there would be no reason to notice it. Along with the asperity goes a honeyed sweetness – which, however, is not just a sweetness of the palate – and a vegetative, damp-straw aroma. All this in a wine which has fruit and flowers, which can be taken young, but which may profitably be laid down for the pleasure of one's grandchildren – and you have a great grape variety.

The wines made from the Chenin Blanc varietal in Vouvray and the middle-Loire are nothing if not distinctive. But beyond their acidity, there is no single, uniquely characteristic flavour, by which we may distinguish them from most or all other wines, as we can, say, Riesling or Sauvignon Blanc. When young, they are delightful; when old – and they can be very old – the acidity preserves the wine and is itself mollified, so that the wine exhibits a richness and complexity of which its youth shows little trace.

Given such a character, it is understandable that wine producers in other parts of the world should plant Chenin Blanc, in the hope of making similar wines. The grape variety is widely planted in South Africa's Cape Province, in California, Australia and (relatively recently) New Zealand. The results have been less than might have been hoped: the grape, when grown in warm climates on good soil, produces generous quantities of good grapes. The wines made from those grapes are, however, disappointing, judged by the standards of the Loire. The wine is crisp, clean and lacking in character. It finds a market as an unexceptional table wine, often mixed with other varieties such as Colombard. Only when the climate in which it is grown approximates to that of the Loire does the grape show any prospect of realising its potential. A number of the New Zealand Chenin Blancs now have the acidity, the fruit, the flowers and the sweet aroma which distinguish their ancestors in Vouvray. It remains to be seen whether they will fulfil in age the promise of their youth.

CABERNET SAUVIGNON

This is the big one. Undoubtedly the best-known varietal name, 'Cabernet Sauvignon' is the designation consumers recognise wherever wine is marketed – and they buy it because they like it. The vast majority know little of its origins, and care less: what they know is that the name on the label guarantees them a wine they know and like. And the guarantee is worth something, which is more than one can say of most varietal names. The Cabernet Sauvignon you buy in an Australian supermarket is recognisably a relative of the Grand Cru from the Medoc. A distant relative, maybe, and not perhaps one which the Girondiste would care to acknowledge socially, but definitely from the same gene-pool.

This grape is one of the most commercially successful cultivars. It is successful, despite its low yield, because it is easy to grow: it will happily tolerate a variety of soils and climates and is little susceptible to rot or mildew. Its harvesting is not critical to its acidity (as in the case with Chardonnay) and, because it ripens late, it has a long growing period in which to concentrate flavours in the fruit. It is successful above all because people like the wines made from it: they enjoy the flavour.

The berry is thick-skinned and its pips are large in proportion to its pulp. Since the pips, together with the skins and the stalks, are the source of tannins in wine, Cabernet Sauvignon wines are high in tannins, both flavour tannins and colour tannins. Indeed, the high tannin content is the key to most of the unique qualities of Cabernet Sauvignon wines. The anthocyanins in the skins are high in those compounds, such as cyanidin and delphinidin, which lie at the blue end of the spectrum, hence the bluish-purple coloration of the young wines.

The tannins are responsible for much of the flavour of the wines: they cause the bracing sensations which attend the consumption of young wines and they are the cause of the depth and complexity which appear in the flavour of the wine as it ages. And Cabernet Sauvignon wines can age like no others. There are plenty of people alive today who have drunk pre-*Phylloxera* (see page 116) clarets with enjoyment. Indeed, for those who can afford them, there are pre-*Phylloxera* clarets to be bought – and if they have been decently cellared, they may still be worth drinking. (Whether they are worth the price they fetch in the market is another matter.)

The tannins are also the reason why Cabernet Sauvignon wines are often blends. In their homeland, they almost always are – blended with Cabernet Franc and Merlot, in a mix which is normally 70 per cent Cabernet Sauvignon and 30 per cent the others, the latter two in various proportions. The fuller, more mellow Cabernet Franc and Merlot fill in the framework which the Cabernet Sauvignon provides, to create a rounder, more satisfying wine, in which the Cabernet Sauvignon tannins are modified in a manner which reduces their impact on the palate and at the same time increases their complexity of flavour.

The tannins also explain the affinity Cabernet Sauvignon has for oak wood. The posher Bordeaux wines are matured in small oak casks for up to two years before being bottled. Small casks are expensive to make and to fill, but the smaller the cask, the larger the surface of the wood which is presented to the wine and hence the higher the extract, so the expense is justified. Such wines, however, are not for drinking immediately: the addition of the oak phenolics to those already in the wine raises tannin levels well beyond what would be pleasant to drink. The wine must be matured in bottle for a decade, or two, or more. As the years roll by, the long, slow polymerisation of phenolics takes place, the tannins become less strident and the complex, fruity flavours of bottle-age replace those of youth. The metaphor for human life is an obvious one, and over-used, mainly by old men. There is some justification for it, though (in the opinion of an oldish man).

The dominant fruity aroma in Cabernet Sauvignon wines is blackcurrant, usually allied to spice and resin of various kinds. As has already been remarked, the source of the blackcurrant aroma has so far eluded the chemists. Since the scent in wine does not emanate from any of the aroma compounds of the blackcurrant fruit, it is to be assumed that either there is some molecule as yet undiscovered which has this effect on our olfactory epithelium, or there exists a combination of otherwise unrelated aroma components which, taken together, have this unique effect. Primary fruit aromas such as blackcurrant are important in the Cabernet Sauvignon wines which are to be drunk young. For those wines which are to be bottle-aged, they are less important, since the primary fruit aromas will be modified and joined in the aged bouquet by other fruit flavours which presumably have a quite different derivation.

After blackcurrant, the aroma most reliably associated with Cabernet Sauvignon wines is the green-grassy group of odours. It seems that these odours are stimulated by growing conditions which are not ideal: either too warm a climate, or over-rich soils, or both. In neither case do the aromas necessarily diminish the flavour of the wine – provided always that they remain at sufficiently low levels. Beyond very low thresholds, however, the odours become obtrusive and wine quality declines

When Cabernet Sauvignon wines are made in places other than Bordeaux, they retain the primary flavour characteristics of the genre, but can throw up all sorts of other flavours. Peynaud lists several of these: resin, cloves, licorice, seaweed, grape stems, industrial fumes and soot. One can see how, given its chemistry, the wine could easily smell of cloves and licorice; grape stems would fall into the vegetative group of aromas; seaweed might derive from the tannins and industrial fumes and soot from sulphur contamination.

The discussion of Cabernet Sauvignon wine so far has focussed on France, for the wines of Bordeaux are the originals of the Cabernet Sauvignon diaspora. While the primary flavours (and most of the secondary) are to be found in most places in which the grape is cultivated, in greater or lesser degree, it should be recognised that some very fine wines are being made outside France, not least in California – wine so good that comparisons with new Bordeaux wines raise high hopes for the future. The best of the Californian wines are being matured in new French oak casks before being bottled. In a decade or so we shall see whether their early promise is realised in the mature wine.

In Australia, Cabernet Sauvignon vines are grown in various places, but the largest parcel by far in South Australia, at Coonawarra. There, very special soils on top of limestone enable very fine grapes to be grown. The Australians understand the importance to Cabernet Sauvignon of blending – only they blend with Syrah, or Shiraz, as it is called in Australian. The Shiraz provides a plummy chocolate filling for the Cabernet Sauvignon cake of good acidity and fruit, to make for a perfectly delicious, if seriously robust, wine.

Cabernet Sauvignon grapes are being grown in just about every wine-making country in the world in which there is a climate which will support them – which means in the great majority. Some very good wines are being made, and some not so good. But one feels – and so it seems do their makers – that every Cabernet Sauvignon wine has at least the *potential* to be great. In other words, the grape is an inspiration to and an aspiration for the people who grow it and make it into wine. This makes a persuasive argument for the vine-centred view of evolution, in which we humans are mere instruments in the march of *Vitis vinifera*.

MERLOT

Merlot is to Cabernet Sauvignon as Semillon is to Sauvignon Blanc: the junior partner in a successful collaboration; the plain companion to the glamorous star. Not quite an ugly duckling, but one which is not worthy of any detailed inspection. For it is noticeable that in descriptions of the blended wines of Bordeaux and elsewhere, the descriptions of flavour are reserved for the Cabernet Sauvignon, while the role of Merlot is to act as the filler, providing 'body' to fill the Cabernet's 'structure', 'richness' to complement Cabernet's nervous elegance.

This seems to be the fate of Merlot almost everywhere: to live in the shadow of its greater associate; to be considered good, but not worthy of detailed description; to make very good wine, but of no *distinction*, in a precise meaning of the word. Almost everywhere, but not quite. On the right bank of the Gironde, in the districts of St Emilion and Pomerol, Merlot finds its apotheosis: the *terroir* in which it flourishes as nowhere else on earth. For on that slope of rich, well-drained soil, wines are made from Merlot grapes of such richness and subtlety that some of them fetch prices which cannot be attained by even the most prestigious of the wines of the Medoc. The wine of Château Petrus is described as strong, rich, fruity, powerful. None of the adjectives says anything which could not be said of a thousand other wines; none of the descriptions suggest that there is anything unique about Château Petrus, save for its assumption of so many excellences in such degree.

Now if we look around us, at the Merlot grape and the wines which are made from it, or in which it is a participant, we find little to suggest that such a thing may be possible. We have already touched on Merlot's junior partnership; nowhere in the descriptions of blended clarets is there a suggestion that Merlot on its own may find such an expression. The vine is planted widely throughout the Gironde, where it covers roughly twice the area given to Cabernet Sauvignon, and in the neighbouring *departements* of Dordogne and Lot-et-Garonne. It is docile and productive and, apart from a susceptibility to frost, is not seriously vulnerable. It is the stuff of many, many wines, most of them good and few of them remarkable.

The grape variety is planted extensively in other parts of France. It is popular in Italy, where it is widely planted and its wines drunk young. It is widely planted also in eastern Europe, in Hungary, Romania and Bulgaria, where it makes some pretty decent wines. It is little-thought of in California, where only a small acreage is planted, while experiments in the northwestern US states of Oregon and Washington have had mixed fortunes. In Australia it is valued by a small band of *aficionados*, but suffers from the success in its potential field of Shiraz

Again we return to the idea that in a certain place or places – be it an individual vineyard or a region – there exists a particular combination of geology and climate such that the balance and concentration of nutrients and micronutrients is by accident fitted perfectly to produce flavour in a particular grape varietal. Hunter Valley for Semillon, Cloudy Bay for Sauvignon Blanc… Château Petrus for Merlot.

SYRAH

Hermitage is the place for Syrah. On this terraced hillside above the Rhône, Syrah grapes are grown which for centuries have produced some of the finest red wines. They were so good that when Louis XIV wished to send a present to Charles II of England it was Hermitage he sent. Charles knew a good thing when he saw it and so did many of his courtiers, so an export market for Hermitage was guaranteed for some centuries to come. By the time critic and historian George Saintsbury was buying his wines in the second half of the 19th century, Hermitage was long-established. It suffered (then as now) from the predominance of Bordeaux and Burgundy, but Saintsbury described a red Hermitage of 1846 as 'one of the three or four most remarkable juices of the grape, not merely that I ever possessed but that I ever tasted'. He goes on to say that when he drank the last bottle of it, the wine was forty years old, at an age at which 'most red wines ... are either past their best, or have no best to come to'. But it had a bouquet 'rather like that of the less-sweet wallflower'.

The grapes used to make Saintsbury's wine were grown on vines which had not yet been afflicted by oidium or *Phylloxera*. The vineyards were slow to recover, for, despite folk like Saintsbury, most of the produce of Hermitage at the time went to Bordeaux and Burgundy, to be blended with the poorer vintages of those regions, to lend them body and flavour. There could be no doubt as to the flavour of the Hermitage wines. Already, tannic wines were aged in new oak, sometimes for as long as six years, before being bottled. Little wonder, then, that after forty years their mellowed contents might still show pronounced and delicious flavours.

There are few wine makers now who will age a wine in new oak for six years, and fewer who will expect to see their wines wait forty years before they are drunk. Syrah grapes from the Rhône are high in phenolics, hence the deep, dark, dense pigmentation. Hence, also, their ferocious astringency when new. But the tannins are the clue to their ability to age. They are necessary, both for the preservation of the wine and for its complexity of flavour when old. Low yields and long, cool fermentation give the Syrahs of the Northern Rhône an intensity of flavour which distinguishes them from the wines of the same grape grown elsewhere in France and in that other bastion of Syrah-growing, Australia. Syrah is now an important grape in the wines of many parts of southern France, where, grown at higher yields, it does not have the intensity of the Northern Rhône, nor the complexity of flavour, but nonetheless produces wines of character and charm.

Syrah, or Shiraz, as it is called in the Antipodes, is the dominant red grape in Australia. It will tolerate the high temperatures to be found in many of the Australian *vignobles* and produce grapes of good flavour at high yields. It is the basis of most of the red wines of Australia, usually blended with another variety such as Grenache. It goes without saying that, in such forms, its flavour is pale by comparison with the great French Syrah wines, but it is not an apt comparison: the Australian Shiraz should rather be measured against the Syrah wines of the Ardèche or Provence, in which case they come out none too badly.

As we have noted, the Australians have taken a leaf from the book of the 19th-century Bordeaux wine makers, and blended Shiraz with Cabernet Sauvignon. While the result is presumably little like the Claret of 150 years ago – though no-one can know for sure – it is one which a great many wine drinkers find extremely satisfying. Like Merlot, the Shiraz provides substance and richness to the more austere Cabernet wines. It also, grown in some of the cooler parts such as southwestern Australia and Victoria, produces a wine which approximates to some of the better qualities of the French model, being dry and peppery, like some of the wines of the northern Rhône.

And in Australia, Shiraz finds a *terroir* which seems to suit it almost as well as the hill of Hermitage: the Barossa Valley vineyards in which Grange Hermitage is grown. Here wines are made which can approximate to the intensity of Hermitage. The Syrah or Shiraz grape has a very long history and is thought by some to have been brought to Europe from its native Middle East by crusaders.

PINOT NOIR

The Pinot Noir, like Chardonnay, is native to the Burgundy region of France, where it is long-established. The Pinot name has been around for six centuries and there is reason to suppose that the grape as we know it was one of the earliest cultivars of the wild *Vitis vinifera*. Various references in Roman times have been plausibly interpreted as being to Pinot Noir. Another indicator of antiquity is the sheer number of variants of Pinot Noir in existence: certainly over one thousand. If only a portion of these can be attributed to the Pinot Noir vine, and the very high mutation rate of the vine is allowed for, the varietal still looks to be pretty ancient.

Like Chardonnay, wines made from Pinot Noir grapes do not have any single signature flavour, but are characterised by a large number of aromas, any of which may be present in greater or lesser degree. What makes the difference between a good Pinot Noir and a poor one lies in the number and intensity of those flavours, and the absence of off-odours. Pinot Noir wines have variously been described as having aromas of raspberries, strawberries, black-currants, violets, plums, game, truffles, cabbages, ink and rotten vegetables. Obviously, some of the aromas are due to fermentation, maturation or contamination, but even allowing for those, we are left with a large variety of primary grape aromas.

The sheer number of clones of the Pinot Noir grape makes generalising difficult. On the whole, the grapes have thin skins and the levels of tannins are low (unlike Chardonnay), so colour is paler than, say, Cabernet Sauvignon or Shiraz, and phenolic flavours are noticeable by their absence. But some clones are in fact thick-skinned and tannic, although these are in the minority, and the low tannins and relatively pale colours can be taken as benchmarks of the Pinot Noir style of red wine.

The low levels of tannins are not the only point of difference from Chardonnays. While the latter variety has gone out from Burgundy to conquer most of the wine-making world, getting Pinot Noir to make decent wine in distant parts can be seriously problematical. Perhaps because of the difficulty, growing good Pinot grapes and making good wines of them has become an ambition of growers and wine makers in many parts of the globe. It is not a rewarding activity, however, for very few Pinot Noir wines made outside France even approach the sheer class of a fine red Burgundy, and most fall far short of it. Pinot Noir buds and ripens early, so spring frosts are a problem. It makes good wine only in coolish climes, which requires the ripe grapes to hang long on the vine, so rot is a problem. Sometimes it is difficult to get the fruit to set at all. And if you survive all that, and you have your harvest of Pinot grapes in good condition, there is no guarantee at all that they will make fine wine in the Burgundian style. Actually, very little chance at all. So we can see why wine makers of a pugnacious temperament regard Pinot Noir as a challenge.

Compared with Cabernet Sauvignon, New World plantings of Pinot Noir are tiny. And many of those are of such a nature as to preclude further investment in the varietal. Pinot Noir grapes in California, with a few honourable exceptions, are rarely recognisable as coming from the same vine as, say, a Romanee-Conti, being dark and tannic, with aromas of plums and burnt cabbage. In cooler climes, however, such as Oregon in the US and Coonawarra in South Australia, Pinots are being made which give some hope of emulating the originals – in relation to medium-quality Burgundies, at least. The top labels would appear to have little to fear as yet. Possibly they may get a fright, though, once some of the New Zealand wine makers turn their attention to Pinot Noir. Growing conditions in some parts of New Zealand are similar to those on the Côte-d'Or – and people who can turn out a Cloudy Bay should be able to coax good wine from a Pinot Noir vine.

Despite its difficulties, Pinot Noir is planted widely throughout Europe, and from Germany to Italy and Romania it produces wines of variable quality and flavour. By far its most important planting outside Burgundy, however, is in Champagne, where, together with Chardonnay and Pinot Meunier, it goes to make Champagne. The black Pinot grapes require to be carefully and lightly pressed in special presses, so that none of the colour is released into the must. The low tannin levels of Pinot Noir skins help here, having low levels of colourings, and those not easily extractable. Most Champagne undergoes a secondary, malolactic, fermentation, which contributes flavour as well as moderating acidity. The practice of blending, however, as well as that of in-bottle fermentation, ensures that it is well-nigh impossible to trace the finished flavours back to any varietal characteristic.

OTHER GRAPE VARIETIES

It would be wrong to leave the subject of grape varietals without mention of at least a few of the hundreds of varieties, others than those mentioned above, which are important for one reason or another. Some, such as Carignan, Aramon and Trebbiano (or Ugni Blanc, as it is known in France) are cultivated mainly for their generous yield, easy growth and resistance to disease. Their wines have little flavour but that, as has already been remarked, is not the point. These are grapes whose wines are produced on an industrial scale, to meet those needs for which industrial production is appropriate. They are the vinous equivalent of the keg beers and ales of the northern world: they are for drinking by people who wish only to quench a thirst cheaply, or who require a substrate which they may distil to make anonymous spirit which can be made to taste by means of synthetic additives.

There are other reasons why low levels of flavour should be desired. Palomino and Pedro Ximenez grapes are used to make sherry. They have low flavour levels though the latter's high sugars make it ideal for sweetening purposes. The primary grape aromas of oxidised wines are a relatively small part of the overall flavour profile, so the absence, in Palomino, of any pronounced varietal character is no great disadvantage. Whenever planted outside Jerez, Palomino grapes produce wines which, being low in sugar and lacking appreciable acidity, are flaccid at best.

But many of the grapes we have omitted from this brief review are varieties which produce varied and flavoursome wines. In the

Riesling mould, we have Gewürztraminer, which has some of the more obvious Riesling flavours, at even higher levels, and Welchriesling, Muller Thurgau and Silvaner, which have them at lower. All make drinkable wines whose flavours are recognisable in a Riesling, but none have the ability to make world-class wines comparable to some of the finest Rieslings.

There are hundreds of Muscat varietals which occupy the flowery-spicy sections of the Aroma Wheel. Some produce sweet table grapes, others make great wines, and there are a lot in between. None, however, produce significantly large quantities of wine. Only one is known for producing wine of quality: Muscat de Frontignan or Muscat Blanc à Petits Grains. (There are lots of other names but they all appear to refer to the same grape.) This variety is grown in Australia and in various parts of Europe, especially in Greece, France and Italy (in the latter, it is made into Moscato, a sparkling wine). The name has a common root in 'musk' and the flavour shares something of that aroma, plus much of the flowery-aromatic character of Gewürztraminer et al. Viognier, which is cultivated in tiny quantities in France (and experimentally in California), has some of the Muscat's flavour spectrum: blossom and peaches without the spice. It makes perfectly lovely wines, and alas is rarely obtainable.

Among red wines, probably the most important omissions are Gamay and the top Italian quartet of Barbera, Nebbiolo, Barolo and Sangiovese. The dark red, ripe-fruit, raspberry, clean flavour of Beaujolais is clearly related to the Gamay grape from which it derives, as are the liquorice and spicy underlay. The wines are for drinking young and are refreshing and toothsome at their best. They have a uniformity of style which makes them easily recognisable. This is not an adequate description of the wines made from the Sangiovese grape, which can produce wonderful, deep, dark wines which will age for a century without loss – and nasty, thin potations whose most valuable characteristic is their toxicity to animal life – and every variety in between. The four other Italians, by contrast, make wines that are almost always of a quality comparable to that of any grape anywhere in the world. Unfortunately, there is a book to be written about each of these – and of course Tempranillo, and so on. All are unique, and the aromas of the grape of each make the wine what it is. If only we knew what they are…

VITICULTURE

Whatever pertains to the growing and harvesting of grapes comes under the heading of Viticulture, literally, the culture of the vine. As we have seen in the preceding chapter, the flavours the grape contributes to the wine vary greatly with the type of grape, and the flavour of the grape depends on the conditions in which it grows and is harvested. Those conditions form the subject of the science and art of viticulture.

The emergence of grape varieties is caused by a combination of mutation and selection, the selection in recent times having arisen from human intervention rather than any natural, non-human process. This selection is an on-going affair, for vines are continually being replanted and only the most promising vines are allowed to propagate. This propagation happens in two ways: sexual and vegetative.

Sexual propagation happens when pollen from the male flower fertilises the female, causing the growth of the seed. Most wild vines are either male or female, with females being in the great majority. For the growth of grapes, pollen from a male vine must be carried onto the flowers of the female. This happens by wind action, or by means of animal vectors, mostly insects. As part of the normal process of mutation, from time to time vines throw up plants which carry both male and female sex organs. These hermaphrodite vines have a much higher rate of successful pollination and hence have been selected (or have selected themselves) as the most suitable for cultivation. Today virtually all cultivated vines are hermaphrodite. The plant propagates sexually when the grape seeds which result from the fertilisation are planted and grow into a new vine which – barring mutation – will be genetically identical to the hermaphrodite parent.

Every gardener knows that many plants will grow from cuttings. If you cut a shoot and either stick it into the ground or graft it onto another plant, it will grow and eventually produce a new plant just like its parent. Most vines are propagated in this way. Because of the incidence of mutation, vines vary a lot, even though they had the same parent and were vegetatively propagated. Some carry better grapes, are healthier, etc., than others. When the grower is taking cuttings, he takes them only from the best vines, hoping that their virtues will be evident in their clones. (It often doesn't work, a fact which seems to have been forgotten by most of the crazies who bang on about human cloning.) In this way, the vines become better and more profitable. (Certainly more profitable: not necessarily better. Superiority is often identified with the heaviest bunches, so clones may be perpetrated whose flavour leaves much to be desired. The Pinot Droit clone of Pinot Noir has resulted in a lot of inferior Burgundies in recent times: it crops heavily but is lacking in flavour.)

Well-managed cloning can improve the vine in many ways. It can be used to produce genetic resistance to disease and it can be used to improve flavour. The latter, however, demands time and effort. Selection for flavour of the grape alone is problematical, and the translation of grape flavours into wine flavours is uncertain. The only way to demonstrate the desirability of any clone, is to cultivate it in sufficient quantity to make wine. The wine must then be judged under the conditions which it will experience in production, which means bottling at least, possibly maturing. The negative cash-flow this involves is unpopular with corporate accountants and growers' bank managers.

Selective cloning is not the only method by which grapes can be improved. Crosses and hybrids can also enhance flavour, yield and disease resistance. Alas, these are subject to the same logic as clones, only on an even longer timescale. Crossing involves the sexual propagation of two distinct varietals to produce seeds which share the genetic material of both. The best-known – perhaps one should say, most notorious – is Muller-Thurgau, a cross of Riesling on Silvaner (or possibly two Rieslings: opinion is divided on this). First produced in Switzerland in 1882, this varietal is now Germany's most-planted grape, and is grown widely throughout eastern Europe and in New Zealand. It has none of the class of Riesling or its ability to age with grace, being deficient in acidity and flavour. It does, however, crop heavily and is more resistant to disease than either Riesling or Silvaner. The rationale for crossing as against cloning is that, since the flavour characteristics of each cross are known, it should be possible to target the desired characteristics more precisely. Unfortunately, this is by no means as easy as it seems, and the cross may possess all or none of the desired attributes.

A distinction is commonly drawn between crosses and hybrids. While a cross is between two varietals, a hybrid is between members of different but related species. There can be some uncertainty here, given doubt as to whether differences in grapes are between varietals or species. In biological taxonomy, two individuals are regarded as being of different species if their offspring are infertile, like mules. This does not seem to be the criterion in most discussion of vines, however.

Interest in interspecies hybridisation blossomed with the great *Phylloxera* plague of the 19th century (see page 116). It was known that indigenous American vines were largely resistant and, over the last century, many hybrids have been produced, with varying results. French- and German-American hybrids are now grown in eastern North America, Germany and England, with considerable success in both the flavour of the wines and their resistance to *Phylloxera*, downy and powdery mildew, and fungal diseases. They are prohibited by the French appellation laws. American-American hybrids, designed to modify the unique and disagreeable flavours of indigenous species such as *Vitis labrusca* and *Vitis rotundifolia* have had considerable success.

The next logical step in the manipulation of the attributes of the vine will be genetic modification. If the *Vitis* genome can be analysed so that the sections which code for relevant functions can be identified, it is a short step to the nipping and tucking which will lead to vines which have all the attributes the wine maker and the consumer can desire. There will no doubt be opposition to this on environmental grounds. But if a vine can be produced which has genetic resistance to disease, then it will be possible to dispense with pesticides and fungicides, and so some environmental trade-off ought to be possible. The problem with this sort of logic seems to be twofold. Firstly, the trade is between a known quantity (the benefits of not using pesticides, etc.) and an unknown quantity (the unverifiable apprehension that genetic modification may lead to unknowable problems in the future). Secondly – related to but not identical with the first – there is the ideological objection, which many anti-GM campaigners appear to have, to genetic modification as a Bad Thing, especially in the hands – as it will probably be – of unrepresentative and irresponsible supranational corporations. This is a big debate, and one which needs more space than it can be given here. However, genetic modification does look very attractive as regards viticulture, so let us hope that the difficulties can be sensibly resolved.

Clonal selection, crossing and hybridisation are not directed to the grape alone, or not directly. The rootstock of the vine is not merely a passive vehicle for the graft. It influences the way in which the vine develops and indirectly how much and what quality of fruit it will provide. Rootstocks vary in their resistance to disease, in the development of their root systems, and in the nature of the vegetative growth of the plant. As is so often the case in making wine, a balance must be struck: too vigorous a rootstock in relation to the soil, and the leaf canopy develops at the expense of the grapes; too weak a rootstock, and there is insufficient growth fully to develop the fruit. The wrong sort of rootstock, and you get disease.

The soil in which the vine is planted has a profound influence on the grapes which are eventually produced. Good wines can be made on a variety of soils, but not normally with the same rootstock or varietal. It is essential to match rootstock to soil if the optimum production of grapes is to be achieved.

After the grape varietal, the two most important determinants of flavour are soil and climate. The term *terroir,* with which we are already familiar, refers to the combination of the two. The word is French. It arose out of observation that one vineyard or group of vineyards consistently produced better wine than did neighbouring vineyards, though grape varieties, viticultural practice and wine-making techniques were identical. This prima facie evidence of difference required explanation, and the concept of *terroir* was coined, partly as a label and partly as an explanation. Its explanatory force was, admittedly, a bit thin.

Terroir has stayed largely a French idea. In Germany, wine makers are much more concerned with climate – not surprisingly, given its crucial importance in such northern regions. If the season is cold in Germany, grape sugars can be disastrously low because the grapes do not ripen – something which happens much more rarely in France. Climate has until recently also been the predominant concern of American and Australian wine makers. Not because of the difficulty of finding a decent climate for growing grapes – quite the reverse: because of the variety of climatic conditions on offer in continents in which land was historically in ample supply, unlike the tightly constricted holdings in Europe.

Terroir seeks to explain the unique. It is not surprising that conglomerate corporate wine makers have little respect for the notion. If you produce decent wine for an international market, and the output of your winery is twenty containers a day, each of which holds one thousand cases of a dozen bottles each, and you get your grapes in tankers trucked from vineyards, some of which are hundreds of miles away, you are unlikely to have much interest in the growing conditions of a patch of land which is a quarter the size of your truck park.

That's OK. Nobody can object to it – just so long as the dynamics of commerce do not lead to a world in which the unique and the individual are subsumed in the uniform and the corporate. Happily, there are enough wine drinkers around the world who have an attachment to the unique for individuality to survive and for individual quality wines to command prices sufficient to ensure that survival. Unfortunately, the corporate intrudes again, for the vineyards which produce the quality wines become valuable commodities in themselves – and when the owners wish to retire, the vineyards are often snapped up by the big corporations. The *terroir* then becomes the property of a public company, the people who work it are the employees of the company, and the connection between the soil and the wine maker is lost. Lost with it is something which is even harder to define. For there is a third component of *terroir*: besides the land and the climate, there are the people. They are the people of the land and, while the land is theirs, there is integration, an identity of interest and of culture. Break that identity, and no amount of science or art will recreate it.

Soils must have adequate supplies of the nutrients the plant requires to grow and to set seed, and for the fruit to develop desirable levels of flavour components. They must not have too much in the way of nutrients, though, for if they do, the leaves of the vines will proliferate at the expense of the berries, and the latter will lack the flavourings required to make good wine. Throughout Europe, vines prosper on soils which will grow practically nothing else. This is very convenient for the Europeans.

The best wines come from well-drained soils with a steady, but not excessive water supply. As elsewhere, balance is everything. If the water supply is inadequate, the grapes will not develop sufficiently, will have insufficient juice for wine making, and may develop water stress. Irrigation has been used since ancient times to make vineyards fertile but there are problems with irrigation as the primary source of water (see below). With too much water, the grapes will develop excessively, and the flavour components which are so desirable will either not form at all or will be excessively diluted by the juice. A moderate supply of water will ensure adequate grape growth, but the growth of the leaf canopy will be restricted and leaf size will be small, ensuring that the plant will not be so shadowed as to restrict its access to sunlight. In such optimal circumstances, berries will also be small, thus ensuring that there is a high ratio of skin to pulp and therefore a high concentration of flavour components. Small berries mean that individual berries are not compressed and have more access to air, which diminishes the incidence of fungal and other diseases – which in turn reduces dependence on chemical fungicides and pesticides.

The chemistry of soil as it affects plant growth is unable as yet to explain much of this in detail. Some of the mechanisms of nitrogen supply are known, however. Excessive supplies of nitrogen lead to undesirable leaf growth, while nitrogen deficiency can result in grapes which are difficult to vinify, since the yeasts which do the job require nitrogen for their metabolic processes. Nitrogen is a component of the all-important amino acids and proteins and an insufficient supply can also lead to stuck fermentation and the production of sulphur-compound off-odours such as hydrogen sulphide and some of the nastier mercaptans.

Supplies are also required of the micronutrients which are important both as flavour components themselves and as vitamins for the yeast growth and reproduction which produces flavours. Copper, zinc, iron, manganese, boron and molybdenum have all been identified as essential, but it is not yet known what their exact function is. The supply of micronutrients is thought to be the reason why extensive root systems contribute to the grapes which make fine wine. It is commonly observed that the best wines come from poor, but well-drained soils in which the roots require to penetrate far and deep in order to find the water and other nutrients the plant requires. Such penetrating root systems pick up large amounts of micronutrients as well as small amounts of water, which leads to a high concentration of flavour components in the grape. This appears to be why the best wines so often come from grapes grown on stony soils. One thinks of the gravels of the Medoc or the stones of Châteauneuf-du-Pape. I recall, on a visit to Château de Beaucastel, being astonished that anything at all could grow in such conditions. No soil is visible at all: only vines sticking up out of a terrain of round river-boulders. But the wine is great.

The presence of stones in the soil – as opposed to on it – is held also to be desirable. The stones diminish the amount of organic material available, thus reducing the supply of nutrients, and improve the drainage. Stones – on the soil or in it – are desirable for their thermal capacity: they store the sunlight during the day and radiate it at night, which is thought to have a beneficial effect on flavour development. Dark soils are thought to be desirable for a similar reason: dark soils absorb more of the sun's heat than pale ones, which reflect it. There has long been a debate as to whether alkaline soils are better than acid ones. There is little evidence for this: good wine is made from grapes which grow in both sorts of soil, provided always that the acidity and alkalinity are not excessive. The adaptation which grape varietals represent appears not to be to soil chemistry, for the same grape will grow pretty well in soils of different pH.

We have established that vines adapt through mutation so as to be able to survive in different habitats. If there is one factor as important as soil in determining that adaptation, it is climate. The principal varieties of *Vitis* represent selective adaptation to different climatic conditions. The Cabernet which will grow so well in the maritime climate of Bordeaux will not prosper on the Loire or in Burgundy; the Pinot Noir which does prosper there is ill-suited to the Garonne. These adaptations are of some antiquity, as was the case with most of the vine varieties of Europe until quite recently.

In traditional viticulture, growers have had to contend with long-term variations in weather. The climate of Europe has fluctuated on both long and short timescales. The period of the Roman Empire was relatively warm, and vine growing spread throughout the Empire, even into northern and western Europe. In the 5th century, temperatures declined sharply and Europe had cold weather for some hundreds of years, so not only did people have to put up with all those barbarians, but they had rotten weather as well. Things got better after a few hundred years, i.e. the weather improved and the barbarians became slightly less barbarous, and by around the 8th century, wine making had been re-established, mainly by the monastic orders who were spreading Christianity. All was well until the late 13th century, when, in addition to the Black Death and the Hundred Years' War, the temperature plummeted. What historian Barbara Tuchman calls 'the disastrous 14th century' saw widespread devastation and weather which would make our worries about global warming laughable. The weather has got better and worse since then on a pretty regular basis, with peaks and troughs about every hundred years until, at the end of the 17th century and into the early 18th, we had a series of terrible winters and bad summers, and there was starvation throughout Europe. Since then, there have been minor fluctuations, but nothing comparable to earlier ones.

The interesting thing is that some of the older varieties such as Pinot Noir – that most sensitive of grapes – survived all the changes. There were bad years, but the vines survived, and well enough to avoid being grubbed up and replaced by something more suited to the then-prevailing climate. We may put this down to the conservatism of traditional vine growers, and the lack of awareness of the opportunities presented by alternative varietals – but this cuts no ice as an evolutionary argument, and the fact is that the genotypes survived. It may of course be that the weather fluctuations, since the 14th century anyway, were of too short a duration to lead to evolutionary change – evolution is, after all, a very slow business indeed.

The grower does not see climate change: what he sees is weather. Weather is climate change on a small scale; only if the weather varies consistently from the norm over a long period, do we say that the climate has changed. The vineyard owner will plant new vines of a different type if he sees he could do better in the market than he has been doing lately. He will take whatever steps he can to cope with adverse weather and replanting is a last resort.

Where consideration of climate rather than weather is necessary, is when a new vineyard is to be made. Then the grower must look at the prevailing climate and consider what grape varieties are likely to prosper. The question is posed in its most acute form when the plantings are to be in distant places which do not have traditional vine varieties, or which do, but ones unsuitable for wine making. In America and Australia, Chile and Argentina, South Africa and New Zealand, this has been the situation. Colonists have had the European vine varieties to choose from and have sought to match variety with climate.

One result of this historical choice has been that growers have brought considerations of climate to an ever-smaller scale, realising that the climate may well vary over quite a short distance. European wine makers had long known about this, especially as regards exposure to the sun. What they had not realised – or had not made explicit anyway – is that all sorts of factors besides sunlight make for variations in climate. The last few decades have led, in the USA and Australasia especially, to a proliferation of vine varietals within quite small areas, each one tailored as closely as possible to the climate – or the prevailing weather – of a particular site. The result has been – despite the conglomerating tendencies mentioned earlier – that in those countries we have seen a variety of wines comparable to that found in Europe.

And events elsewhere in the world have had a knock-on effect in traditional wine-producing areas of Europe. Universal education and mass media have meant that peasants' children are aware of what is going on in the rest of the world, and the children have asked why their parents do not grow grapes which can make wines which can be sold beyond the confines of the locality. In many places they have grubbed up the traditional vines and replanted with vines better suited both to the climate and to the requirements of the national and international marketplace. This has had good and bad effects. It has meant a loss in individuality on the one hand, with distinctive local varieties being replaced with the big international types. On the other, it has led to some perfectly delicious wines being produced in places which previously had not figured on anyone's wine map.

Climate for grape growers means three things: temperature, rain and wind. Two kinds of climate produce grapes suitable for making wine of quality: the maritime-to-continental climate of western and central Europe, with its cool growing season followed by summer rain and moderate ripening temperatures; and the Mediterranean, in which the heat of dry summers is ameliorated by cool sea breezes, and irrigation supplies any deficiency of rainfall in the growing period. There are of course all sorts of gradations between the two. Wines can successfully be grown in a climate which generally is too cold, provided that the prevailing microclimate in the growing area is warm enough. By the same token, careful canopy management can shade grapes in hot climates and allow grapes to ripen satisfactorily even though temperatures are well above the ideal. In cold climates, sugar deficiency is the most common problem and in hot climates acidity deficiency. Both of these can be rectified in the course of vinification, by adding sugar (chaptalisation and its equivalents in countries other than France) and acid. The laws of most wine-producing countries prohibit the simultaneous employment of both.

Low temperatures during the growing season restrict the growth of the vine; low mean temperatures in the ripening period (below 19 °C for white and 21 °C for reds) prevent the conversion of acids, so the grapes will be sour. High temperatures in the ripening season use up valuable sugars as energy to support the transpiration necessary to maintain the plant's internal temperature and fluid balance. At mean temperatures a few degrees higher than 21 °C, this will cause sugar levels to fall appreciably and the resulting wines will be lacking in alcohol and, because enzyme activity depends on the availability of sugar, flavour compounds as well. (Phenolics are synthesised from sugars by the activity of enzymatic reactions, which work best in the

20–24 °C temperature range.) Higher temperatures cause reduced levels of malic acid and hence deficiencies in the total acidity of the grape. There is a slight but real conflict in temperature requirements: the optimum temperature for sugar and malic acid development is a degree or two lower than that for anthocyanins synthesis. Hence in an ideal world, harvesting should take place when ripening has been followed by a spell of cooler weather.

High wine quality depends not only on growing and ripening temperatures, but on the amount of temperature variation. All vineyards vary in temperature, from day to day and from day to night. The best have the least variation: the factors are microclimate, topography, soil type and soil cover. If night-time temperatures are in the 15–20 °C range, photosynthesis appears not to cease with daylight, but to continue to create flavour and colour compounds.

Once the grapes have reached a certain level of maturity (the change of colour in black grapes), the more rapid the ripening the better – for sugar, colour, acidity and flavour in general. This is one of the areas in which the vine variety matters, for different varieties will tolerate widely differing conditions. Riesling, for example, will attain full flavour maturity while still at acid levels which in another variety would indicate that the grape is unripe.

Extremes of climate are to be avoided, since damage to the grapes or the vine can occur if temperatures are too high or too low. In spring, the main danger is from frost: like any other plant, the vine is vulnerable to damage by frost once spring growth is under way, and serious frost damage will cause cell damage and can kill or distort buds. In either case, fruit setting will be impaired and the crop of grapes diminished in both quantity and quality. Grape varieties vary greatly in their tolerance of frost. As you would expect, those which do well in northern climes, such as Riesling, Gewürztraminer and Pinot Noir, have greatest genetic resistance to frost damage. Excessive heat, on the other hand, can damage leaves and scorch grapes. Neither is much good for the plant and, together with the defects of too hot a climate, will seriously diminish grape quality. (Photosynthesis and hence sugar production drops sharply with rising temperature: the rate at 35 °C is only some 15 per cent of what it is at 25 °C.)

Direct sunlight is desirable as part of the overall temperature equation. It is also instrumental in promoting bud and flower growth, fruit maturation and the development of aromatic compounds in the fruit. It is therefore very important for the flavour of the wine. Buds which are exposed to a lot of sunlight develop more flowers than those which are not. Since the fruit develops from the flowers, that means more grapes. Fruit which is exposed to the sun normally has lower levels of potassium and malic acid, has smaller grapes, and has higher quantities of tartaric acid and anthocyanins. Since tartaric acid is less tart than malic, such grapes will taste less sour; since anthocyanins are precursors of flavour compounds, they will have higher levels of the minor flavour components.

Where direct sunlight is not, curiously, effective, is in photosynthesis. The ultraviolet part of the light spectrum active in photosynthesis comes to the vine directly as direct sunlight and indirectly as diffused sunlight. (The latter is caused by the sun's rays diffusing in the atmosphere. When you have to wear sunglasses to drive on a day when there is no direct sunlight, it is diffused light which causes the problem.) Diffused light penetrates more deeply into the leaf canopy because it comes from all angles. The vine will synthesise as much sugar in diffuse as in direct sunlight and, because it does not have to expend energy in maintaining its temperature through transpiration, and the temperature generally is likely to be lower, the sugar levels at the end of the day will be higher.

The largest part of the water a vine draws from the ground is used in maintaining its temperature, by evaporation from the leaves. Rainfall as such is not essential for viticulture, since vines can be grown wherever there is sufficient groundwater. Rain is, however, desirable if quality wines are to be made from the grapes, and it is apparent that the very best wines tend to come from areas where there is relatively high humidity and fairly low rates of evaporation. The most desirable arrangement is for rain to fall early in the growing period and for ripening and harvest to take place in warm, dry conditions. Early rainfall promotes budding and fruit setting, while late rainfall brings about excessive vegetative growth, diverting the resources of the plant away from the accumulation of sugars and other flavour components in the grape. Rain and no sun at the start of ripening is worst of all, for the flavour quality of the grapes will be poor. Heavy rain close to maturity is almost as bad, for that can cause physical damage to the ripe fruit and, because the grapes are by then closely bunched, create the conditions for fungal infection.

Wind as well as rain brings problems for the vine grower. The two together can cause serious physical damage to both vines and fruits. Wind can do likewise. Strong winds combined with heat cause problems associated with excessive evaporation. In dry conditions, too high a rate of evaporation will cause the rate of water loss to exceed the rate of replenishment via the roots. In those conditions, the plant's pores will close, cell temperatures will rise and cell metabolism will slow down. This obviously will diminish both the plant's ability to produce fruit and the desired flavour components of what fruit it does produce. In extreme conditions, the temperature of the cells will rise beyond the point at which metabolic activities can be maintained and the cells will die – and with them the plant. Irrigation is the answer, together with canopy management, which, by shading, allows the rate of evaporation from the lower leaves to be much less than it is from those exposed to sun and wind.

But irrigation is a controversial subject. (There is very little to do with wine making which isn't.) So controversial, indeed, that the French appellation laws prohibit it throughout most of France. Happily for France, there is very little need for it there, whereas in countries such as Australia, Chile and Argentina, vine growing without irrigation would be impossible. Since the latter countries produce good wines, it cannot be doubted that irrigation in certain circumstances is a good thing. The problems arise because it means that the growing conditions of the vines are in even tighter human control, and, humans being what they are, the temptation to use irrigation to maximise yields will rarely be resisted. Where the object is to produce white wines destined to be consumed young and cheaply, there can be no objection, for irrigation together with ample sunlight and good soil will produce large, juicy grapes of low acidity. Properly vinified, they yield decent, if undistinguished, wine. The levels of fruity flavours will be low, and they won't age well, but those things don't matter for the market in view. Red wines present much more of a problem, for, as we have seen, red wines get most of their flavour components from their skins. If the ratio of skin to juice is low, as it is in large, juicy grapes, then the levels of flavourings will also be low. The wine will be deficient in the essential tannins and acidity, and will lack flavour in youth and in age. There are various forms of irrigation, which range from the broad brush of flooding the entire vineyard to the fine point of drip-feed, which gives each vine its own individual, controllable supply. Irrigation can allow vines to grow – and therefore wine to be made – which without it would not be possible. To that extent it is undeniably a good thing. Used with judgement, irrigation can allow good wines to be made when without it the wine would not be good. For that reason, too, it is a good thing. If some people use it to make a buck by growing grapes which will produce cheap wines, that's no reason to condemn it.

Soil and climate are the objective conditions for vine growth and fruiting. Given those conditions, vines will grow and grapes will be there for the picking at harvest time. But for an optimum yield of grapes of good quality for wine making, a lot of human intervention is necessary. This intervention can take many forms. Irrigation we have already mentioned: since it involves an alteration of the objective conditions, it ought strictly to have fallen into this section. Besides giving the plants the right amount of water, there are two things you have to do to get good grapes: you must get rid of or prevent bugs and other diseases, and you must prune the vines. (There are various other things you may choose to do, such as working the ground between and under the vines, but they are not commonly thought to be strictly necessary.)

Disease control is of the utmost importance. Some pests can be killed directly, others, like viruses and some bugs, can be controlled only by selection of resistant rootstocks. The great *Phylloxera* plague which struck the vines of Europe in the later 19th century was caused by a bug introduced from America, where it was endemic. It devastated the European (and later other) vineyards. Nobody was able to devise a way of killing the thing, so the only way to deal with it was to use rootstocks which had a natural immunity – which meant the American vines, which had evolved in coexistence with the bug for so long that they had mutated so as to be resistant to it. Most wine in the world is now made from European grape varieties grafted onto American *Phylloxera*-resistant rootstocks. From the vine's point of view, it means that its natural vectors, humans, have adapted sufficiently to provide it with an environmental niche which allows it to flourish.

The later-19th century was a worrying time to be in the wine business. On the one hand, there were some wonderful vintages – in the twenty years up to 1880 there were no fewer than seven truly great vintages. There were good markets for the wines of those years and even the lesser years were easy to sell because of the general confidence and publicity produced by the great years. But there were all sorts of nasty things creeping and crawling into the heart of Europe's wines, which were to devastate wine production throughout the continent: oidium, downy mildew, fan-leaf virus, leaf roll… No wonder some people thought that a golden age was ending and that the new century heralded a time of trouble. They were right, as it turned out, but not for the reasons they thought, and none of them had much to do with wine. But for wine, there was to be a half–century of misery, collapsing markets and changing attitudes. The middle classes in Britain ceased to drink anything but fortified wines, and the Americans banned liquor altogether.

The French addressed themselves to the problems with a typically Gallic mixture of bad policy and good science. A dusting of powdered sulphur put paid to the oidium, which raised hopes and brought lots of kudos to the scientists. So did their remarkably prompt discovery of the cure for downy mildew, in the years following its appearance in 1878: lime mixed with copper sulphate. Both those cures were to introduce rather large amounts of sulphur into the vineyard. As we have seen, sulphur is not a nice thing to have incorporated in your organic molecules, for it gives rise to thiols and the like, all of which taste and smell very nasty. Surprisingly, the flavour effects were very slight and the scientists gained in credibility. They needed any gains they could get in that department, for they were to be found wanting when it came to the virus diseases and above all, to the *Phylloxera*. For, as we have seen, the only cure to *Phylloxera* turned out to be the introduction of American rootstock into Europe and the grafting onto it of the European vines. Unfortunately, the rootstocks carried other viruses…

'Balance of nature' is a phrase which has rather gone out of fashion. It was used to describe a situation in which various organisms manage to coexist by living off each other, or on each other, or just in proximity to each other. Each organism occupies whatever space the constraints of the habitat allow and symbiotic relationships are established, often of great complexity, in which all the members of a biosphere impinge in one way or another on all of the others. The processes of random mutation and natural selection work to ensure that each critter does the best it can, but there are checks imposed by the environment which ensure that no one species takes over the whole show. So in America, the *Phylloxera* bug developed a taste for vine roots over the millennia during which the vine developed a tolerance for *Phylloxera*. When the two were introduced into Europe, however, the balance was upset, for we had a voracious pest meeting a host which had no resistance. The solution was of course to introduce hosts which had resistance. Only nobody realised that those hosts were carrying lots of other organisms, among them various viruses. But at least the *Phylloxera* was done for.

Except that, remember, every species from time to time throws up a mutation, and some of those mutations do rather well. In the monoculture which is a vineyard, mutations proliferate unnoticed until they become evident by their inability to resist a pest to which they had been thought immune. Thus we find that in various places, both in Europe and America, *Phylloxera oxera* is again appearing. Whether this is due to a weakening of the immunity of the rootstocks or to tougher *Phylloxera* bugs is not yet known. No doubt once it is, someone will think of a way round the problem, and the wheel will turn again. And then there are fungal pathogens, and Eutypa dieback, and Black Rot, and Crown Gall, and Pierce's Disease, and Yellows Disease, and Yellow Speckle, and Root-knot nematodes, and Dagger nematodes, and Leafhoppers, and Torticid Moths, and Spider Mites and a few other minor nuisances, and of course variants on all of them, so the vine grower does not lack for interest in his or her chosen profession.

When the viticulturist is not dealing with pests, he or she can concentrate on managing the vines. Vine management is necessary to optimise yield and flavour from the vines, and to cope with the minor variations in the growing conditions in the vineyard. By far the most important aspect of management is the pruning of the vine. Pruning involves physical alteration of the tissue of the vine so as to optimise grape quality and quantity, and to achieve the desired balance between the two. Pruning reduces the ability of the vine to produce fruit. It does this by removing the buds which will form into fruits and by cutting out tissue which contains stored nutrients. There must be a balance in this as in all things to do with wine making: too little bud removal, and the vine will produce an excessive amount of fruit of poor flavour; too much tissue excision, and the vine will have insufficient resources fully to mature what fruit it does set. So the lack of flavour in your wine may be due to either too much or too little pruning. What is more, if the pruner gets it wrong, the capacity of the vine will be reduced for several years to come.

There is a balance to be struck between the fruit and the leaf canopy, for there must be enough leaves to provide by photosynthesis the sugars and flavour components the fruit requires if it is to make good wine. Given even a moderately fertile soil, pruning for leaf cover reduction is necessary, otherwise there will be too much vegetative growth. But the pruning must be done with a light touch, otherwise the grapes will not ripen sufficiently. In that case, the trick is to thin the bunches of immature grapes to just the right extent.

If the vine has too many shoots, the available nutrients will be too thinly spread, so shoots must be pruned, leaving only an optimum number to bear the fruit. Again, the pruning must not be too severe, or there will not be enough shoots to carry all the fruit of which the vine is capable and valuable capacity will be lost.

Besides its direct effect on grape quantity and quality, pruning indirectly affects the juice of the grape. The timing and extent of the pruning will influence the timing of the breaking of the buds, and thus the ripening of the grapes. A harvest in which all the grapes are ripe will result in a better wine than will one in which a large proportion of the grapes are unripe, or rotten. The degree and timing of pruning must be related to the weather, the fertility of the soil, the nature of rootstock and cultivar, and several other factors. It can be seen then, in that case, the judgment as to when to prune and by how much is a fine one. The management of the vineyard is consequently extremely important in the production of good wine.

Decisions on pruning must also take account of the vine shape most suited to the conditions, as well as the economics of harvesting. The ancestral vines almost certainly were climbers which used trees and bushes as support. This is still the case in much of Italy and Portugal, where vines are grown on trellises, or on fruit trees, often with crops planted in between, in whatever polyculture is best suited to the demands of the local economy. This is essentially a peasant mode of production, maximising the return from the land irrespective of quality of product or the input of labour required. Only once wine is made in a society with a degree of specialisation of function, do we find dedicated vineyards – though in recent times, in societies as specialised as the USA, there has been a return to polyculture of a sort, usually for environmental reasons.

The shape of the vine is determined by a combination of the local growing conditions and the method of pruning and harvesting. Trellised vines arranged in hedges with broad spaces between are ideal for machine pruning and harvesting. Closely spaced bush vines are much more difficult to mechanise, so that form tends to be grown where vines are still pruned and grapes still picked by hand. The shape of the vine has little influence on the flavour of the wine, provided that the pruning is done in such a way as to ensure the proper balance of vegetation and berries, and sufficient exposure to sunlight for the required level of sugar synthesis.

Harvesting is mechanised in all industrial-scale wine production. The harvester bestrides the rows of vines, at night in warm climates, removing the bunches and transferring them to a hopper, from which they are discharged into a truck which takes them to the winery. There is no subtlety and stalks and leaves go in along with the grapes. The stalks and leaves are normally separated before the grapes are crushed, though the separation is often fairly inefficient, ensuring that the raw tannins of leaves and stalks are embodied in the wine. At the opposite end of the scale is the harvest of the best wines, in which bunches are picked by hand and transferred with the greatest care to the crusher and the press. Some of the most expensive wines – top Sauternes and Trockenbeerenauslesen – pick individual berries in order to ensure only the very best fruit finds its way into the press.

It goes without saying that the differing techniques and values of harvesting are reflected in the quality of the wines. The tannins in Grand Cru Bordeaux reds are very different from the tannins in their cheap and distant cousins from the torrid zones of Australia, despite the use of the same grape varieties. Those differences, as we have seen, are due to a great many causes, of which the harvesting is only one, but an important one. There is a two-way tension between the market value of a wine and the production values embodied in it. Wines which fetch a high price are wines the producer will take great care of, for if he does not, the price will fall. Conversely, but not invariably, high production values bring high prices. In a perfectly rational market they certainly would but, as we all know, markets are rarely rational and never perfect. As long as that continues to be the case, some wines will be sold for much more than their flavour warrants. The corollary of this is that some wines will be sold for much less. Thus the imperfection of the market is the connoisseur's opportunity to drink well at modest cost.

FLAVOUR ORIGINS
≈VINIFICATION≈

In the preceding chapters we have looked at how your wine gets its taste from the grape, and at how what happens in the vineyard affects the flavour of the wine made from the grape. In this chapter, we look at how the harvested grapes get to be wine, and at how what is done to them in the process affects how the wine tastes.

The elements of alcohol production are always the same, no matter what it is made from. Sugar is fermented by yeast into alcohol. People made wine from grapes long before they made beer from barley, for the simple reason that with grapes you have ready-made sugar, whereas with barley and all other cereals which store their energy as starch, you need to break down the starch polymer into its sugar fractions before you can begin. What is more, in making wines you don't even need to add yeast. There are lots of different sorts of yeasts. They are microorganisms so small that they are invisible to the naked eye unless there are huge numbers of them, in which case they look like mud. They are ubiquitous in the environment (i.e. they are all around us); they float about and when they land on anything they can feed on, they multiply prodigiously. When your beer goes bad or the food you left in the kitchen starts fermenting and smells funny, yeasts are usually to blame.

Like most critters, yeasts are terrific breeders, given the right circumstances. With a plentiful supply of sugars, an aqueous medium and a moderate temperature, yeasts will produce a population explosion which makes rabbits look like nuns. Like all other vital processes, this population explosion requires an energy supply and the energy supply, like all other biological energy supplies, is based on burning sugar. Ethanol and carbon dioxide are by-products of the sugar burn.

While the grape is growing in the vineyard, passing yeasts land on its skin and stay there. When the grapes are harvested, some of the skins break, releasing the juice. The resident yeasts immediately begin work on the juices, and start the fermentation which is to convert them into wine. Since, as we shall see, the wine maker requires to have all his grapes ferment simultaneously if he is to avoid undesirable flavours, the grapes are transferred as rapidly as possible from vineyard to winery. In traditional peasant or bourgeois wine making this presents few problems, for the winery is the farmhouse or château and is hard-by the vineyard. Where wine is made on an industrial scale, grapes are often transported by truck over large distances, so refrigeration is required, to slow down the process of fermentation.

Premature fermentation is not the only risk attendant on the breaking of grape skins. Whenever skins are broken, or even damaged by bruising, the juice is exposed to atmospheric oxygen and the process of oxidation begins. We are all familiar with what happens when you slice an apple. After a very short time, the flesh of the apple begins to go brown and if left alone it will quickly rot. The browning is the result of exposure to the air, and consequent oxidation. The same happens to grapes and if there is more than a very small degree of oxidative browning, both the flavour and the colour of the wine will be affected. What is more, yeasts are not the only visitors to populate the skins of grapes. Lots of bacteria find a comfortable home on grape skins and are consequently well placed to feast on the juices released by the breaking skins. The results of this bacterial fermentation show as various flavour components which are not required, to put it mildly.

Once in the winery, the grapes are crushed and the yeasts begin their work. The rate of fermentation depends on the temperature and on the strains of yeast present. In wine making on any scale other than that of the peasant, cultured yeasts are used in addition to the natural fauna of the grape. (I say 'fauna' rather than 'flora' because, while yeasts are not clearly either animal or vegetable, in the present context they lean toward the animal, in that their main food is sugars and their by-product carbon dioxide.) The use of cultured yeasts allows the wine maker a degree of control over the fermentation and so allows him or her to influence the flavour of the resultant wine.

LEAVES AND SKINS

But we are getting ahead of ourselves. Before the grapes get to the fermentation stage, there are several factors which can radically affect the flavour of the finished wine. The most important of these is the presence of stems and leaves in the fermenting wine. We have mentioned the phenolic flavour components (tannins etc.) which are extracted from the skins of the grape, and which are so important in the colour as well as the flavour of red wines. Leaves and stems are also powerful sources of phenolics. If the stems and leaves find their way into the fermenting vat, the alcohol in the wine will extract large amounts of leaf and stem tannins. In the making of white wines, which are mostly very low in tannins, this is especially to be avoided. In red wine-making, too, it is rarely desirable, for the phenolics contributed by stems and leaves are very different in kind, and therefore in flavour, from the tannins which come from grape skins.

Leaf and stem tannins have a much more bitter and astringent taste than skin tannins. The flavours mostly have their source in six-carbon alcohols and their aldehydes which enzymes produce from linoleic and linolenic acids. They give the finished wine a grassy, herbaceous odour. In some wines, this is acceptable up to a point but above pretty low limits it comes across as an off-note. Fashions change, and such flavours are less acceptable today than once they were. In traditional wine making, leaves and stems went through the whole of the fermentation process and the resultant wines were much more bitter than the same wine would be today. When the peasants who picked the grapes were the same folk who dumped them into a tun and then got in beside them to tread them down, you can be sure that a lot of stems went in as well. You can also be sure that a lot of the folk who did the treading didn't bother to wash their feet first, on the cogent ground that the best way of cleaning your feet is to tread grapes. I know people who, challenged as to the hygiene of this practice, point out that nobody ever died of it and, anyway, it makes the wine taste better. Both assertions are very likely true: the former because of the antibacterial action of alcohol and the latter on account of the beneficial influence on flavour of minuscule amounts of various interesting compounds found on sweaty feet.

In contemporary wine making, there are three circumstances in which stems and leaves may intentionally be left in the must during fermentation. One is where a tannic wine is demanded of grapes whose skins are not naturally high in tannins. The natural tannins are augmented by leaf and stem tannins. The resulting wines may have the required levels of phenolics, but they rarely attain the flavour quality of wines whose tannins come from the skins. The second circumstance is in the case of a poor vintage in which cool weather and insufficient sunshine have produced tannin-deficient grapes. The wine, though the colour may be fine, will not taste as nice as it would were the tannins obtained from the skins alone. The third circumstance is where carbonic maceration is employed and whole bunches of grapes, together with attached stems, go into the fermentation vat. We shall come to this shortly.

There is an argument for retaining stems in the mix: they prevent the pressed mass of skins and pips becoming too compact for juice to pass through. Less pressure is accordingly required and it takes less time to complete the pressing, so there is less opportunity for tannin extraction. The balance of opinion, though, is that unintended pressing of stems leads to unwanted phenolics.

DE-STEMMING AND CRUSHING

As soon as the grapes reach the winery, they are de-stemmed and crushed, and this is generally done by the same machine. De-stemming usually consists of passing the grape bunches through a drum which has holes big enough for the grapes to fall through, but not the stems. The bunches are propelled along the drum by a series of paddles, which break off the stalks. This cannot be done without breaking some of the grapes, so crushing normally takes place immediately so as to minimise the influence of oxidation.

Various machines have been devised to crush grapes: by passing them through rollers, by pressing them against the sides of a perforated drum, by centrifuging them. The main requirement is to avoid crushing the seeds, whose tannins are much more bitter than the skin tannins. The traditional peasant method of crushing by treading with bare feet was very effective, for human feet are not hard enough to break grape pips – or to crush stems, for that matter.

Some wines are not crushed before being pressed, besides those in whose making carbonic maceration (see below) is to be employed. Where white wine is to be made from black grapes, the grape clusters are generally pressed intact, so as to minimise the contact of juice with broken skins and consequent extraction of the anthocyanins which give colour. This is commonly the case with sparkling wines made from Pinot Noir grapes. Botrytized grapes (see page 92), too, are often pressed without prior crushing, so as to diminish the incidence of fungal polymers which clog filters.

When grapes are crushed, a large part of the juice runs out directly. This, the free-run juice, is the juice contained in the middle parts of the grapes. It has very little contact with grape skins, seeds or stems and tends to be low in phenolics and high in other flavour compounds. The free-run juice is very different in character from the remaining juice, which is extracted by pressing. The latter has much higher levels of phenolic flavour compounds and is regarded as being of lower quality than the free-run juice. In a few wines of very high quality and low tannins, only free-run juice is used. Normally, though, the free-run juice is mixed with the juice from the press. The proportions of this mix determine the quality of the finished wine.

MACERATION

Time matters. The longer the crushed grapes are left immersed in the free-run juice, the more phenolics will be extracted from the skins, etc. This is not merely a process of dissolution: the ruptured cells release enzymes which facilitate the release of flavour and colour compounds from the skins and seeds of the grapes. The timing and temperature of maceration determine the flavour of the wine. White wines which are required to be drunk very young and whose character is to be fresh and lively, spend very little time in contact with the skins. The juice is run off immediately and the remaining materials are pressed gently, so as to minimise colour and tannin extraction. Temperatures are kept very low. The amounts of phenols extracted at this stage depend to a great extent on the grape varieties. The skins of Sauvignon Blanc and Palomino grapes release very small amounts of phenols; Chardonnay, Riesling and Semillon very high.

Phenols are not the only flavour compounds extracted by maceration. Skin contact increases the levels of a great many other flavours as well. This process is enhanced if the juice is briefly heated. The trick with this is to be able to do it without increasing the uptake of phenolics. Warmer maceration leads to higher levels of colour and more complex flavours. The duration and temperature of maceration is consequently an important tool which the wine maker may employ in shaping the character of his or her wine.

Maceration is what allows red wine to develop its colour and many of its flavours. Red wines employ much longer macerations than do white. Where the maceration is less than 24 hours, rosé wines are the result. Rosé wines are rarely of great character. They show few of the flavour compounds which develop in whites, while the short maceration period does not allow them to develop the depth of colour and flavour we find in red wines.

Red wines which are to be drunk young are normally macerated for three to five days. This is sufficient time to allow them to develop a good colour and flavour, but is not sufficient to allow the uptake of phenolics which we find in the red wines which are capable of ageing with grace. It is not uncommon for red wines of high quality to be macerated on the skins for two weeks or more.

125

As with white wines, the rate of flavour extraction is proportional to temperature. There is a recently adopted process known as cold maceration, which is employed with Pinot Noir grapes, which involves a period of a few days' maceration at low temperatures prior to fermentation. This enhances colour and contributes to a greater intensity of flavour. It appears that science has just discovered the natural conditions which obtain in some of the caves of Burgundy, in which Pinot Noir grapes have been made into wine for some time by people who just did what they could and found they got decent wine.

Carbonic maceration is a technique employed only in making red wines and involves harvesting grapes in intact bunches and transferring these, unbroken, to a fermentation vessel. The vessel is first flushed with carbon dioxide at atmospheric pressure, which expels all the oxygen from it. The grapes die because of the lack of oxygen and the natural processes of decay which follow death begin. The enzymes within the grape attack its sugars and convert them to alcohol *inside the intact grape*. This goes on, at a relatively high temperature, for between five and fifteen days, at the end of which time the grapes contain about 3 per cent of alcohol. The juice is then run off, the must pressed, the two combined and cooled and then run into the fermentation vat, where they are fermented with yeast in the usual way. The cooler second fermentation yields many of the fruity flavours which are desired in a wine intended to be drunk young, while the first stage has extracted sufficient of the colourant phenols for the wine to have a deep colour. Hence Beaujolais Nouveau, which has both good colour and fruity flavours at a very early age.

Beaujolais and Beaujolais Villages wines are made by a technique which is halfway between carbonic maceration and the ordinary method. This involves the use of open vats, into which whole bunches of Gamay grapes are put. The weight of the grapes above crushes those on the bottom and causes their juices to flow. The yeasts on the skins work on the sugars in the juices, causing a normal, aerobic, fermentation which produces alcohol and releases large amounts of carbon dioxide. Because carbon dioxide is heavier than air, the vat fills up with the former, pushing the air out the top. The unbroken grapes are then immersed in carbon dioxide and a carbonic maceration begins. The resulting wine is the highly distinctive Beaujolais.

PRESSING

There is a big difference between red and white wines in the matter of pressing. Because as little skin contact as possible is required, grapes for white wines are usually pressed as soon as they have been crushed. Indeed it is common in white wine-making for the same machine to crush and press. The juice from the press is run off and clarified by allowing particulate matter to settle. Once this has taken place, the juice is racked off into clean vats. Some wine makers use a centrifuge to separate the juice from any bits of skin, etc. This is very efficient: indeed, a little too efficient for some, for it removes yeast cells as well as other particles. This is convenient if a cultured yeast is to be used, for it removes the uncertainties which the presence of wild yeasts inevitably creates as to when the fermentation will happen and for how long.

With red wines things are a little different. The crushed grapes go directly into the fermentation vat: juice, skins, pips and any other matter which has escaped the de-stemmer. There the grape yeasts, helped if necessary by cultured yeasts, commence the fermentation in the presence of skins et al. In addition to the enzymatic extraction of flavour compounds, there is an alcoholic extraction, as the alcohol produced by the fermentation increases in strength. Carbon dioxide produced by the fermentation is trapped under the grape detritus, which floats to the top. From time to time this cap is punched down into the fermenting liquid to ensure that as many as possible of its flavour components are dissolved in the juice. Flavour component compounds are created by the action of yeasts on grape sugars, by the extraction of phenolics from the skins, by the operations of enzymes and by the enormous number of interactions involving original components and synthesized compounds. No wonder the flavour of wine is sometimes complicated.

The fermented product, now describable as wine, is run off from the fermenting vat. The mass of grapes, or pomace, is then pressed to extract any of the wine which may still remain. This press wine is much higher in tannins etc. than the free-run wine, and the two are generally mixed. In white wine production, the free-run juice is normally mixed with the first pressing: subsequent pressings being too high in phenolics for the wine of high quality. Riesling grapes are an exception: later pressings of Riesling grapes contain high concentrations of the terpenes which contribute to the varietal aroma, so wines made from that grape commonly contain higher proportions of late-pressed wine than is the case with other varietals.

The earliest recognisable press is the basket press: the familiar drum of vertical staves of wood, in which the pomace is squeezed by the descent of the lid and the press wine runs out between the staves.

In mediaeval versions of this press the lid is forced down by a simple lever, on the end of which are hung stones, or anything suitably heavy. The lever arrangement was very effective, but difficult to control. As soon as people discovered how to cut a regular helix on a piece of hard wood, which was in the late mediaeval period in most of Europe, a screw replaced the lever. The vertical screw press became the standard method until the 19th century, when technology began to intrude on traditional practices. That said, the makers of many of the finest wines still use screw presses. The disadvantage of the screw press is that it requires the wine maker to exert a great deal of force, which breaks the pips and releases their tannins into the wine. An early development which obviated this was the very simple device of increasing the area of the press. The larger the diameter, the less pressure is required to squeeze the pomace; the less the pressure, the fewer broken seeds and the less tannic the wine.

The practicalities of constructing and operating a press limit the expansion of its area. An ingenious device permitted an extension of the technology, by simply arranging the press horizontally and having both ends move inward, driven by a single screw. Then the limit imposed by the height of the press disappears and it is possible to squeeze large quantities of pomace at low pressures. What is more, the pressure can be varied to suit the grape variety being pressed and the quality of juice required from it. In some versions of the press, chains are stretched between the plates and compressed along with the pomace. When the plates move apart, the chains are pulled horizontal, which causes them to break up the mass of skins etc. ready for the next pressing. Horizontal screw presses are still widely used and produce wine of high quality.

Pneumatic presses also use a horizontal cylinder – the middle of which is occupied by a rubber bag. The grapes are loaded in the top, which is closed, and the bag is inflated, crushing the grapes against the perforated sides of the cylinder, through which the juice escapes. This press, too, yields juice or wine of high quality by using very modest pressure to achieve a very complete pressing.

The problem with all the presses described is that they involve discontinuous processes, having to be loaded, pressed and emptied. Such devices are ill-suited to the requirements of industrial-scale production, which demands continuous processes. The continuous press consists of an Archimedes screw within a cylinder. The screw is fed grapes from a hopper and as the screw moves the mass along the tube, the juice or wine is squeezed out. The pitch of the screw diminishes gradually towards the far end, so that the mass is squeezed into an ever-smaller volume and the pressure increases proportionately. By arranging the collection at various points along the screw, different qualities of juice can be obtained. The earlier the collection, the better the flavour characteristics of the juice.

MUST CLARIFICATION AND ADJUSTMENT

At this point, before the commencement of fermentation (with any luck), there is the opportunity to make adjustments which will affect the flavour of the finished wine. The first adjustment, in the case of white wine only, is clarification. The must as it comes from the press is cloudy, due to the presence of particles of solid matter left by the very partial filtration provided by the press. If these solids are left in the must during fermentations, various unfortunate consequences for the flavour of the wine ensue. The formation of higher alcohols is facilitated by the presence of particles: higher alcohols are associated with a loss of fruity flavours and so are undesirable. Particles of more than a certain size are also associated with enzyme-catalyzed oxidation, which spoils flavour, and the formation of hydrogen sulphide, which is one of the most offensive off-notes in itself and, being highly reactive, a most powerful producer of associated malodorous compounds.

Various means are used to remove particles. The traditional method is simply to allow the solid matter to stand and settle. Since the particles are only slightly denser than the liquid in which they are suspended, this takes rather a long time, which brings dangers of oxidation and of yeast and bacterial activity. To combat these, the must is cooled and treated with sulphur dioxide. The length of time taken to settle can be shortened by treating the must with bentonite, a clay made up of hydrated oxides of aluminium and sodium. This is *fining*. The clay disperses in the must and the clay particles attract the particulate must material, which sticks to them. The clay with bits of must attached is denser than the must and so sinks quite quickly. It is a simple and efficient process, but its use is contentious, for it can remove many of the fatty acids which contribute to the development of flavour in the wine. It does however, remove most of the polyphenoloxidase enzymes, which cause the must to oxidise, so also impedes the formation of off-notes.

Centrifuging is an efficient and controllable method of removing particles. It too has disadvantages, though, for it can induce undesirable oxidation if not carefully used. And by removing the very finest particles, it can deprive the yeast of nutrients which are essential for fermentation. Flotation is a gentler method – nitrogen bubbled up through the must takes the particles with it to the surface, where they can be skimmed off.

Besides clarification, certain alterations can be made at this stage which greatly improve the chances of the must turning into decent wine. Of these, the best-known and most influential is the addition of sugar. This takes several forms, but whatever its form, the result is the same: an increase in the alcohol level of the finished wine. This is the only consequence of such additions, since all the added sugar is converted to alcohol and none of it remains available for sweetening the wine – or at least that's what we are always told. If one looks at the mechanisms which determine the residual sugar in a wine (the principal cause of sweetness), it seems a little improbable that none of the residual sugar will be attributable to the sugar added. One suspects that the frequently made assertion about added sugar owes more to successful propaganda on the part of the European wine industry than it does to any scientific evidence.

In most European wine-producing countries other than Spain, Italy and Greece, the sunshine in an average year is insufficient to ripen grapes fully. That means, among other things, that the grape will have more acids and fewer sugars than it would in ideal conditions. Less sugar means less alcohol and wine which is not as good as it might be. By the end of the 18th century, French wine makers had realised that their wines could be improved by the addition of sugar before fermentation, though the mechanism by which this improvement was effected was not known. Jean-Antoine Chaptal was a chemist with an interest in wine. In 1801 he published the *Traité Théorique et Pratique sur la Culture de la Vigne*, and in 1807 *L'Art de Faire le Vin*. He recommended the addition of grape sugar to wine must and, if grape sugar was not available, beet or cane sugar, as a way of improving the vast quantities of inferior wine which at the time were being made in France. When he became Napoleon's Minister of the Interior, he was in a position to do something about it and the practice of adding sugar to musts was adopted throughout France. It became known as chaptalisation and there can be no doubt that the wines of the 19th century and after tasted a whole lot better because of M. Chaptal.

Like everything else to do with wine, chaptalisation is controversial. Lots of wine makers employ it and say nothing. It is legal in almost all of France, in Germany and Austria and various other, mostly northern, countries, although the term 'chaptalisation' is out of favour in France and the practice is now generally referred to as 'enrichment'. Besides increasing the alcohol content (which in itself improves the flavour of wine), chaptalisation increases levels of glycerol, 2,3 butanediol and succinic acid, all important flavour components. In Riesling grapes, it diminishes the green-fruit, unripe components. Unfermented, concentrated grape juice is generally preferred as an additive, since it is closer to the real thing and its sugars are glucose and sucrose, as they are in the grapes from which the wine is made. Sugars derived from beet and cane, on the other hand, are mostly sucrose. But the sucrose is broken down by the acids in the must into glucose and fructose, so it doesn't seem to make much difference. Any way you look at it, the practice gives us drinkable wines where without it we would have thin, acid potations. If folk who make wine in hot countries – where the grapes have no shortage of sugar – look down on it, well, they would, wouldn't they?

The acidity of a wine is certainly at least as important a component of flavour as sweetness. As we have seen, grapes grown in good soils in warm climates tend to be deficient in acidity: flaccid and lacking the zest which is one of the desiderata of good wine. Grapes grown in a bad year, or in a climate too far to the north (or to the south in the southern hemisphere) will often turn out to be too acid as well as lacking in grape sugars. Most wine-making countries permit adjustment of the pH of the wine must prior to fermentation. Some permit it after, others do not. It is better done before, when it can be effective in limiting the growth of microorganisms. De-acidification is normally carried out after fermentation. In principle, such adjustment is pretty simple: if there is insufficient acid, you just add some; if the wine is too acidic, you add some alkali to neutralise some of the acid.

No doubt, if you have followed the argument so far, you will not be surprised to learn that it isn't that simple. For a start, you can't use any old acid or alkali, for different acids and alkalis have very different flavour implications. The acids permitted are those which are found naturally in the grapes: tartaric and malic acids. Both are available in pure form. Tartaric acid is preferred because malic is liable to be broken down in a subsequent malolactic fermentation, which we shall look at later. Citric acid is another possibility, but little used because of its susceptibility to yeast metabolism, which turns it into acetic acid – which of course causes volatile acidity, which nobody wants. The addition of any acid is permitted only in the hottest parts of Europe and the use of citric acid is banned in Europe, though permitted elsewhere.

De-acidification is carried out by adding chalk – calcium carbonate – or potassium carbonate, which are both mild alkalis. The addition of chalk reduces acidity by converting the tartaric acid into the calcium salt, calcium tartrate. This works fine in reducing acidity, but it causes problems because calcium tartrate is soluble in wine and only slowly crystallises out – typically after bottling, when it produces a sediment which leads to ignorant customers sending back their wine. Potassium bicarbonate is preferred as a de-acidifier, because the resultant salt, potassium bitartrate, crystallises out at low temperatures and so may be removed by cooling. A double salt of calcium carbonate and calcium tartrate-malate is sometimes used. It is effective in that it removes both malic and tartaric acids. It is, however, too expensive to be widely used.

Besides the adjustment of sugars and acidity, the addition of trace nutrients is generally permitted by governments concerned for the quality and authenticity of their countries' wines. Nitrogen is required as a yeast nutrient for the formation of amino acids. Since atmospheric nitrogen is not accessible, nitrogen in the form of ammonium compounds is added when must nitrogen is deficient. This is normally only required in the case of botrytized wines (see page 92), or white wines which have been over-clarified, so that fermentation will not start.

FERMENTATION

At long last we get to the bit which really does the business: the fermentation of the must into wine. The term 'fermentation' is used to describe a wide range of biochemical reactions, bacterial as well as fungal. (Yeast is classified as a fungus, having much in common with mushrooms and dry rot, though its operations are rather more beneficial to humans than the latter. It resembles mushrooms in being an important source of flavour in its own right and in conferring flavour on the fluids in which it acts, such as putative wine and beer.) The fermentation with which we are concerned at present is the alcoholic fermentation in which yeasts consume sugars and produce ethanol and carbon dioxide, as well as a whole lot of minor metabolites which contribute to the flavour of the wine. Bacterial fermentation is brought about by the action of bacteria rather than fungi. The malolactic fermentation is a bacterial fermentation and we look at this on page 136.

When yeast comes in contact with the sugars in the grape, it uses those sugars to fuel its reproduction. If sufficient sugars are available, the numbers of yeast cells will increase exponentially until the increase is brought to a halt by some external constraint. If an adequate supply of oxygen is available, the end result of the yeast activity will be carbon dioxide and water. In the first stage of fermentation, oxygen is available, so the rate of increase of yeast cells is prodigious. Wine makers commonly aerate the must just before fermentation to ensure that it has enough oxygen to generate the explosive expansion. Oxygen is normally the enemy of wine, but at this stage it is beneficial, and it is soon used up by the yeast.

Once the oxygen supply is used up, the yeast is unable fully to metabolise the sugar and, instead of water, it produces ethanol.

From one sugar molecule you get two alcohol and two carbon dioxide molecules. This is a lot of carbon dioxide: in small wineries it simply escapes to the air; in large ones it is collected and compressed for industrial use. Carbon dioxide in any concentration is highly toxic to humans and care must be taken to remove it. As everyone knows who has sniffed a vat in turbulent fermentation, a good lungful of carbon dioxide can knock you off your feet.

Ethanol is central to all liquor production: in moderation its intoxicating effects make us feel good – but possibly more importantly, at least as regards wine, we value it for the flavours which accompany it or in whose production it plays a part. There are such things as non-alcoholic wines but they are poor potations, which lack flavour as well as the ability to intoxicate.

We are not alone in having an alcoholic limit, beyond which we cannot function. Yeasts, like folk, slow down, stop working and eventually die when their ethanol passes a certain point. Like folk, different yeasts have different tolerances: some stop soon, others can keep going much longer. The variation in tolerance is one of the factors which determine how much sugar will be left in a wine once fermentation has stopped. A strong yeast will keep going until almost all the sugar has been consumed and converted to alcohol; a weak yeast will succumb and cease to function long before all the available sugars have been converted.

There are lots of different species of yeast and each grape will normally harbour a number of them. The most important yeast in wine making is without doubt *Saccharomyces cerevisiae*, a species widely used by humans but which seems rarely to occur naturally as part of the grape flora. Yeasts, being unicellular creatures which reproduce in enormous numbers, readily throw natural mutations. These mutations often differ significantly from their parents and it is this difference which gives rise to the many strains (as the variations are known) of *S. cerevisiae*. Different strains of the yeast are described as baker's yeast, brewer's yeast, distiller's yeast and wine yeast. Their biological origin is not known, but is thought not to have been the grape.

In traditional wine-making, fermentation is caused by the action of naturally occurring yeasts. Species such as *Kloeckera apiculata* and *Candida stellata* compete for dominance. *K. apiculata* grows initially, producing glycerol and various esters as well as ethanol. After a few days it weakens and *Candida* takes over as the dominant genus. *Candida* is a large genus of fungi, which will be familiar to female readers in a quite different context. Both *Candida* and *Kloeckera* are fairly resistant to ethanol, but neither can compete in this regard with *S. cerevisiae*, which, if present even in minuscule quantities, will soon take over as the dominant species. *S. cerevisiae* also creates an environment hostile to most bacteria, so concurrent bacterial fermentation is impeded, with the possible exception of lactic acid bacteria.

This is very fortunate, for *S. cerevisiae* produces numerous flavour components in addition to ethanol. Higher alcohols, fatty acids, esters and aromatics all owe their presence to this yeast fermentation or to the alcohol which it produces. In most wine making today, *S. cerevisiae* is inoculated into the must, where it soon establishes dominance over the indigenous species. (It may, of course, be present anyway, for its use in wine making means that it has become part of the natural flora of most wineries and, through the use of grape detritus as fertiliser, of vineyards.

Since yeast species and strains differ greatly in the conditions they will tolerate, the use of cultured yeasts gives the wine maker yet another way of controlling fermentation. If he or she wishes to induce fermentation in cold conditions to augment the fruit flavours of the wine, there are available species such as *S. uvarum*, which will tolerate low temperatures and will produce abundant fruity esters as well as glycerol, succinic acid and higher alcohols. *S. uvarum* will also convert malic acid and produce very low levels of acetic acid, so is a good thing. Variant strains of *S. cerevisiae* are available which will cope with most wine-making situations. It is, however, becoming understood that the indigenous yeasts may make important contributions to flavour, either directly, or by producing precursors which the dominant yeast converts to desirable flavour components.

Once fermentation has commenced, it is not an easy matter to stop it without destroying the wine. The main instrument is temperature, for yeast, like other organisms, will slow down if it gets cold.

Fermentation is an exothermic reaction, so produces its own heat. Anyone who has been close to the vat when fermentation is in progress will be in no doubt of that. In traditional wine making, which took place in the cool autumn, cooling was normally not a problem. Small casks offered a large surface relative to volume, which allowed heat to escape. When wine is made in industrial quantities, however, and especially if it is made in a warm climate, some method of cooling the fermenting vat is needed. If the temperature rises too far, many of the most desirable flavour components will be lost and their place taken by flavours which are far from desirable.

The technology of cooling is well developed and normally consists of a refrigeration plant which passes cool brine or ethylene glycol solution through pipes which run through the fermenting must. This arrangement, allied to the luscious fruit which is typically produced in warm climates, is responsible for some of the banana- and pineapple-estery flavours which in recent times we have seen in lots of greenish wines from such places.

Red wines are usually fermented at temperatures considerably higher than white. Given the much higher rate of extraction desired of red wines, this is understandable. Fortunately the flavours which are generally considered desirable in a red wine are also generated at relatively high temperatures.

There is a great variation in fermenting techniques and vessels between traditional and industrial wine making. The latter, which takes its grapes in truckloads, requires enormous vessels with all the attendant technology. In the former, the scale of vinification is appropriate to the tiny quantities involved. In a top-quality vineyard in Burgundy or Bordeaux, separate fermentation is essential to preserve the individuality of very small parcels of land. When the grapes from that parcel are picked in bunches or even individually (as with Trockenbeerenauslese and other botrytized grapes), the quantity to be vinified becomes smaller still. When quantities are small and products are of a premium nature, the selling price of the wine as well as the requirements of scale will support fermentation in small barrels. With white wines in small barrels there may be a loss of fruity flavours due to fermentation temperatures higher than would be the case in controllable stainless-steel vessels. This loss, however, may be more than offset by the acquisition of barrel-related flavours of greater depth and subtlety than those lost, and of a character which will permit ageing, and the development of yet another layer of flavour.

The wood of the fermenting barrel contributes directly to the flavour of the wine. Polyphenols of various sorts dissolve in the alcohol and take part in fermentation and subsequent reactions. The yeast, too, interacts with the wood components, producing further levels of flavouring components. The wine maker can exert a certain amount of control over this, by care in the choice of barrel. He or she can specify the region from which the staves are cut and therefore some variation in the wood chemistry. Most casks are charred prior to use and the degree of charring affects both the nature and the amounts of flavouring compounds. By specifying the degree of toast, the wine maker can ensure that the cooper provides a container whose active chemistry is appropriate to the wine which it is to contain.

Once the fermentation is over, the wine maker has the option of drawing the wine off directly, or of leaving it on the lees (sediment). In the latter case, the wine will continue to acquire desirable flavours – but at a risk, for after a little while the oak flavours may give way to off-odours generated by residual action of the yeasts.

MALOLACTIC FERMENTATION

This is the secondary, bacterial fermentation which may take place after the primary, alcoholic fermentation has ceased. The action of lactic acid bacteria causes the very sharp-tasting malic acid to be converted into the less-sharp lactic acid, together with the release of carbon dioxide.

In wines which are excessively acid, malolactic fermentation is highly desirable. Not only does it diminish the sharp taste of the wine, but along with the emollient effect goes a noticeable improvement in other aspects of flavour. Vegetal, herbaceous flavours are diminished and fruit flavours increased. Malolactic fermentation is most common in red wine-making. Tartness is replaced by soft, supple flavours which complement the other flavours of the wine so that a wine which before was harsh, can become very pleasant indeed. Some white wines, too are encouraged to undergo malolactic fermentation, though care must be taken to avoid the danger of the wine losing what character it has and gaining little in its place.

Paradoxically, the wines which most need malolactic fermentation are those in which it is most difficult to induce it, and those in which its induction is easy are those in which it is undesirable. Lactic acid bacteria function best in relatively warm conditions of low acidity. Alas, such conditions favour the production of wines which are low in acidity and which, if they undergo malolactic fermentation, lose what acidity they have and become flat and unattractive. Conversely, in cool climates which produce acidic wines, it is difficult to start secondary fermentation. In traditional wine making in Europe, malolactic fermentation would normally begin in the spring after the vintage, as cellar temperatures rose.

There are various lactic acid bacteria, of which the most beneficial is *Leuconostoc oenos*. You may recall an earlier discussion of the attribution of species to variations in biological types. *Leuconostoc* is a case in point: after many years of being a species of the genus *Leuconostoc*, *L. oenos* has now been allocated a genus of its own and the designation *Oenococcus oeni*. So much for the rigours of taxonomy.

Among the many other bacteria – some related to *L. oenos*, some not – are some which, besides the principal reaction, generate unpleasant flavours. *Lactobacillus* and *Pediococcus* are two of the worst offenders in wine making and where they have been active wine is generally spoiled. Diacetyl is one of the most common flavour consequences of such malolactic fermentation. In small quantities it can give a toasted, buttery flavour, but above a low threshold it is disagreeable. Cheesy, milky odours are particularly associated with lactobacilli where the wine is insufficiently acid to begin with. Amines, too, may be synthesised by some lactobacilli in conditions of insufficient acidity. Acetic acid production is another hazard and of course it brings with it the likelihood of ethyl acetate.

It will be apparent that malolactic fermentation is not without its hazards. It remains nonetheless an important source of desirable flavours in fine wines. The application of science has reduced the uncertainties of traditional wine making and allowed the wine maker to choose whether or not the wine shall undergo malolactic fermentation. If it is desired, he or she can warm the wine and inoculate it with the best strain of the best bacillus; if not, the solution is simple: keep it cool.

FLAVOUR ORIGINS
≈ELEVAGE≈

levage is the French term used to cover everything which happens to wine once fermentation has stopped. A pretty close English equivalent is 'upbringing'. Like most people, few wines are naturally good: they require to be well brought-up if they are to reach their full potential. Immediately after fermentation has ceased, the wine is drinkable, but along with the fresh fermentation aromas there come lots of flavours which require to be modified or removed. The wine must be raised to maturity before it can show what it is capable of. It will most likely require adjustment, blending, stabilisation and clarification. It will need some time to mature: how long depends on the nature of the wine, for, again, wines are like people – some are precocious, others want time to develop and fully realise their potential. Typically the best of them are the latter, though the former have their uses.

ADJUSTMENT

Wine making is not an exact science; before the fermentation, it is difficult to predict exactly the character of the fermented wine. As we have seen, adjustments of various sorts are generally permitted prior to fermentation. Despite such adjustments, though, the fermented wine may turn out to be deficient or overloaded in various ways, for the agents at work in the wine may act in unforeseen ways. *Saccharomyces cerevisiae*, for example, in addition to producing alcohol, may bring about the creation of significant amounts of malic acid. If this occurs, and the must acidity has been correctly adjusted prior to fermentation, the pH of the wine is likely to be much too low. In most European jurisdictions, that's just too bad, and post-fermentation adjustment is not allowed. (Which is not to say, of course, that is does not happen.) But some wine-making regions and countries permit post-fermentation sweetening and acidity adjustment. The techniques are broadly similar to those which apply before fermentation, with the proviso that any sweetening must be done with great care and in sterile conditions if the sugars are not to ferment in the bottle. Various methods are available to effect adjustments, ranging from the simple addition of tartaric or malic acid for increasing acidity, to ion exchange techniques for reducing it.

STABILISATION AND CLARIFICATION

As we have seen, after being pressed, the must is clarified before it goes into the fermenting vat. By the time the fermentation has ceased, the wine is anything but clear: indeed it may be positively muddy. Its liquid content is now a mixture of water and ethanol; suspended in the liquid are dead yeast cells, dead bacteria, fragments of grape cells, precipitated tannins and various crystallised salts. Not only does it not taste nice, it looks terrible and, as every wine merchant knows, nobody will buy a wine which doesn't look right. The wine maker must, therefore, do whatever is necessary to produce wine which is perfectly clear in the bottle, and preferably leaves no sediment at the bottom. This must be done with as much care as was taken to make the wine in the first place, for each step in improving the appearance and flavour of the wine is fraught with possibilities for its destruction.

Some of the methods by which the wine is clarified are very similar to those which were applied prior to fermentation. Filtration is widely employed as a method of removing suspended solids: not only particles which can be seen, but also entities too small to be detected by the naked eye but big enough to be trapped in a filter. This means, at the lower end of the scale, all microorganisms whatever – yeasts and bacteria included. A wine which is this finely filtered will be perfectly sterile and stable even if sugar is added. It is also unlikely to be more than a little lacking in flavour, for filtered sterility is not a condition in which one finds wines of the most generous or subtle flavours.

That said, filters have a part to play in making good wines. Wines – white wines especially – which are intended to be drunk young, require to be stabilised quickly and in big batches. Filtration is the way to do it. The wine is passed through progressively finer filters until it is perfectly clear and (hopefully) stable. The flavours which most appeal in young, white wines are those unlikely to be stripped out by any filter: the fruity, flowery, acidic flavours of New World Semillons, Rieslings and Pinot Blancs, as well as the grassy, green notes of Sauvignon Blancs.

Various sorts of filter are employed in wine making; provided they do the job they are intended to, they have little significance for flavour. There are two main types: depth filters and surface filters, each of which is capable of different arrangements. Depth filters are those in which the fluid passes through a considerable depth of filter material, leaving particles trapped in the passages of the filter. Asbestos was widely used for this, and was very effective, but has now been banned. Cellulose is now mostly used in its place, normally in the form of paper pads through which the filtrate must pass and in which it leaves the larger particles. Paper filter pads are capable of catching very small particles, but the finest depth filters are those which employ diatomaceous earths such as kieselguhr. This is a mineral mined in Germany which is the fossilised remains of diatoms, tiny sea creatures which lived millions of years ago. This earth is processed and cleaned, and the remaining material used to trap the very finest of particles.

Surface filters take the form of perforated membranes whose perforations are smaller than the particles to be removed. The fluids can pass through, but the particles are caught. Filters of this sort quickly clog up, as the particles become embedded in the pores of the filter. They are accordingly used only for the final stage of any filtration. It is essential that whatever filter material is used, it be completely inert. (There is little point in filtering out noxious substances only to replace them with equally unpleasant stuff from the filter.) Calcium and metal contamination occasionally result from filtration, as do papery odours. The first wine through the filter is sometimes kept aside, to ensure that it is not contaminated.

The clear-filtration to which most modern wines are subjected does not, alas, ensure wine in bottle which is perfectly free from any sediment or cloudiness. The most common cause of the former is the formation of crystals of potassium bitartrate. We looked at the flavour implications of tartaric acid in Chapter 3 and at how both potassium and calcium form tartrate salts. These reduce the acidity of the wine by converting tartaric acid into the flavour-neutral salt. Grape must is normally a saturated solution of potassium bitartrate. The salt is less soluble in alcohol than it is in water and so the formation of alcohol in the must causes crystals of the tartrate to form. Filtration can remove the crystals, but can do nothing about the salts which remain in solution. This creates a problem once the wine is bottled, for precipitation in the bottle gives rise to crystals which grow until they can look like broken glass. (I have actually seen a bottle sent back in a restaurant by a diner who insisted that the bottle had broken glass in it. No amount of assurance by the sommelier would convince him of the contrary.)

The normal cure for the problem is to chill the wine before bottling to a temperature lower than any it is likely to encounter thereafter. Since solubility diminishes with temperature, any tartrates will precipitate at the lower temperature and the wine will be stable in bottle. In northern wine cellars, this often occurs naturally, as temperatures drop in winter, but in warmer wine-making regions it can be a serious problem. Nor does cooling always do the job: the presence of suspended colloids (large protein molecules) in the wine can retard the deposition of bitartrate crystals during cooling, leaving them available to crystallise later. Seeding with tiny crystals prior to cooling can help with this, since crystals form much more readily if there is something for them to form *on*, and the minute crystals provide that substrate.

Calcium tartrate crystal formation is much less common than potassium crystals. This is fortunate because chilling does not cause the salts to precipitate out. De-acidification with calcium carbonate as well as seeding with calcium tartrate crystals is usually necessary.

Protein haze is another manifestation of instability in wine. Dissolved proteins cluster together, becoming visible as a slight haze once the clusters pass a certain size. The solution to this is fining. Fining is an important weapon in the battle for clarity in wine. It is inexpensive and for most wines is perfectly satisfactory. There are implications to its use, however, for it can remove flavour as well as colour. Thiol varietal fragrances, as found in Sauvignon Blanc wines, are especially vulnerable.

We mentioned bentonite in connection with the clarification of juice. It performs the same service for the fermented wine and is one of the materials most commonly used as a fining agent. The molecules of this clay carry a negative electrical charge, which causes them to attract the positively charged protein molecules. The clay-protein clumps are sufficiently dense to sink in the wine and form sediment, from which the wine can be racked off (see page 142). If there is any difficulty in getting the clumps to settle, they can readily be removed by centrifuging. As well as removing protein haze from wines, Bentonite is also effective in removing some metallic contaminants. It is cheap and effective; it settles rapidly and is easily filtered. It does cause some colour loss, but its effects on flavour are

141

minimal compared with those of other fining agents. It consists mainly of aluminium silicate and when soaked in water it expands so much that one gram provides a surface available for adsorption of seven to eight hundred square metres!

Various other fining agents are used to clarify wines. Albumin, the protein of which egg whites are mostly composed, is relatively common, though much more expensive than bentonite. It is generally employed for removing excess tannins from red wines. Gelatin is used for the same purpose. It is a protein related to albumin which is obtained by boiling up the bones and hides of animals. This activity, which is extremely malodorous, produces a pure, clear protein which is useful for fining both red and white wines, from which it removes large phenolic molecules. Casein, a similar protein derived from milk, is used likewise. Isinglass, the protein of fish swim bladders, will take tannins from white wines, though its use is becoming limited due to a shortage of sturgeons, the principal source. Tannins themselves, obtained from oak galls and combined with gelatin, can be used to remove colloidal proteins from wine. Charcoal, in its purified form of activated carbon, is an effective fining agent which will remove both colour and off-odours from wine. Unfortunately, activated carbon can contribute off-odours of its own and can also remove many desirable flavour compounds.

The traditional method of clarifying wine is also one of the most effective, both as regards the final stability of the wine and the absence of side effects. Racking, as it is known, consists of simply leaving the wine in the barrel after fermentation until the sediment (lees) settles; then drawing as much wine as possible off into a clean barrel. The wine is drawn only until sediment begins to come over. A number of casks are racked at the one time and each newly filled cask topped up until there is no air space.

The wine is often left on its lees for several weeks before racking takes place. If malolactic fermentation is to be encouraged, the racking is left until the secondary fermentation is complete. Leaving the wine on its lees can produce improvements in the flavour of the wine, as flavourants are extracted from the lees.

There is presently considerable interest, mainly in North America, in maturation on the lees, a procedure which previously was mainly to be found in connection with the white wines of Burgundy and some of those of the Loire. Some white wines left on their lees in small barrels for three to six months acquire valuable flavour characteristics. Nutrients and aromatics transfer from the lees to the wine. Enzymes in the lees cause the release of aromatic flavour compounds which previously were present only in bound forms, which prevented their flavours from becoming evident. There is, as usual, a price to pay. The sediment will produce reduced-sulphur off-odours unless it is regularly stirred and aerated. The oxygen taken up during this process can lead to the growth of acetic acid bacteria, so sulphur dioxide is required to prevent volatile acidity. And wines matured *sur lies* are susceptible to sunstruck odour or *gout de lumière* (see page 153–54).

Racking contributes to the stability of the wine by removing bacterial cells and nutrients which bacteria might utilise. In the first racking, most of the yeast cells are removed, as well as dead bacteria and fragments of grape cells. Subsequent rackings will remove any remaining bacteria, tartrate crystals, precipitated tannins and fining sediment. If racking is done carefully, it can result in a wine which is perfectly clear and stable. It is, however, labour-intensive and requires considerable skill and organisation. Until a century ago, this was the only method of clarifying wines. There can be no doubt at all that it works and that it does not have any seriously undesirable flavour implications. It prevents the formation of undesirable, reduced-sulphur compounds by stirring up the lees. While developed for wines in small-scale cooperage, racking lends itself to wine making on an industrial scale, when the process can be mechanised and indeed computerised.

BLENDING

When wine is produced for domestic consumption, or is to be sold on to a commune or a big buyer for bottling in bulk, the vintage will simply be bottled or shipped out in its natural condition. But where the wine is intended to be sold in a market under its own unique label, things are very different. To understand what happens to the wine then, we must know a little about markets and how producers relate to them.

Almost everyone who makes wine which is to be marketed under a label, does it in the expectation of a return. For a few wealthy amateurs this return may take the form of esteem, either their own or their peers'. But for the vast majority, the return which matters is money, and that is what separates the amateur from the professional. In wine making, as in some other pursuits, there are wealthy individuals for whom the status is more important than the money. Such people are often content to make huge losses year after year in pursuit of excellence – and good luck to them: there are a lot worse things they could do with their money. But the true professional doesn't take such folk seriously. He or she makes wine to make a buck and profit is the most important criterion of success.

Wine is like any other commodity: the buyer must be persuaded of the value of the brand. All goods sold in an international market (and in very much smaller markets, too) are sold with reference to a recognisable brand identity. What the customer buys is the brand first, commodity second. The decision to purchase is made because the brand is perceived as being desirable and the desirability of the brand may or may not be related to the utility or other value of the commodity. Lots of people buy lots of things solely on the basis of their associations and not because of any value in the goods. At the time of writing, the international drinks market is flooded with alcoholic drinks aimed at young drinkers, who buy the drinks purely because they are persuaded by advertising of the desirable associations of the brand. In the trade press, drinks' company executives admit this freely. 'Sure,' they say, 'It doesn't matter what the stuff tastes like: it's the brand that matters.'

Wine is a very varied commodity. A few wine makers operate on a scale large enough for them to create brands based solely on associations. But the market is very fragmented and, by and large, people's attitudes to wine are a little more mature than the kids' attitudes to alcopops. It is probably true to say – and indeed it is the basic premise of this book – that most people approaching a bottle of wine do so in the expectation that they will enjoy the taste. If they do, they will identify the label – the brand – with that enjoyment and they will buy the same label again. The flavour and the label are then amalgamated in the brand identity. This is exactly what every wine maker is seeking. Such identification is the basis of his or her business, be it Leoville-Barton or the local supermarket's cheapest.

Branding makes two demands of the wine maker. Firstly, he or she must make wine whose flavour is such that the customer will enjoy it and will buy the brand again; and secondly, having achieved the first, the wine maker must ensure that the quality of the brand (and hence the consumer's experience) does not vary between the first and subsequent bottles. Only if both those conditions are met, can a wine brand be successful.

This brand logic is the same for wines as it is for any commodity. The matter of vintages complicates things a little, since a wine by its nature is a natural product and consequently liable to seasonal fluctuation. But vintages in fine wines are for the few: the international wine market has been built on uniform products suitable for mass-consumption. The vast majority of wine drinkers the world over expect their favourite wine to be the same irrespective of occurrences such as poor weather – or, for that matter, natural calamity. And the power of the brand, as represented by the label, can transcend even the variability of good and bad vintages. For the label of a fine wine stands as an assurance of quality: not of absolute quality, but of quality relative to others of the sort, and to the year's weather.

Which brings us to blending. The wine maker, producing wine for sale, must decide what flavour the wine is to have. If the business is larger than just a few fields, there is likely to be more than one variety of grape at the wine maker's disposal. And some vineyards will produce better grapes than others. Some parts of the same vineyard may do consistently better than other parts. When the grapes are pressed, the free-run juice will be less tannic than the pressed, and when they are fermented, the wine from one vessel which is wooden will be different from that from the new stainless-steel fermenter. And if the new wine is to be left in oak for a while, won't that make a difference, too? So even at quite a small scale, the wine maker is faced with a wealth of choice as to what sort and quality of wine should be bottled under his or her label, in order to meet the expectations which previous bottlings have raised in the customers. Those expectations are met by blending.

After the wine has been racked once, it will be tasted, and its flavour assessed. An experienced wine maker can see through all the extraneous tastes and aromas to the probable flavour of the finished wine. It is at this point that decisions must be made as to which wine will be blended with which, in order that the quality and character of the wine bottled under the label may be as consistent as possible.

Apart from the effects gained by leaving wine on its lees, there are two main post-fermentation stages in which some wines improve their flavours. These are both, in the general meaning of the term, maturation, for they both refer to relatively slow processes by which off-notes are gradually lost and pleasant flavours gained. We are talking here of the period the wine will spend in a wooden cask, and of the time it will remain in bottle. Some wines will gain greatly from both; others will gain by neither. This is the point at which the distinction is made between fine wines and those which are of lesser quality. Fine wines will benefit from ageing and ordinary wines will not. In fairness, it has to be said that this proposition is more a value judgement than an empirical observation. There can be no doubt that the facts underlying it are true: that certain wines with certain characteristics gain in their typical flavours on being left in wood and bottle, and others, the majority, do not. The former are by definition fine wines and the latter not. The definition is one made by folk who like the fine wines better than the others. It is also fair to say that the people who appreciate the less-than-fine wines are in the great majority.

CASK MATURATION

The timber used for casks is mostly oak, though other woods, such as chestnut and acacia, are sometimes used. No other woods have the physical and chemical properties of oak, however. Trees of the genus *Quercus* are found throughout the world and are valued almost everywhere for their unique properties. New oak is easy to cut and it can be shaped with ease by heating it. This allows it to be made into containers for fluids, a purpose for which it has been employed for two, possibly four thousand years. Barrels may seem to the modern eye most unwieldy and illogical in shape, for we are accustomed to containers of regular shapes – which are dictated by the economics of the packaging industry and made possible by advances in technology. It is worth remembering that glass bottles came into widespread use only about three hundred years ago in advanced countries such as France and Britain. In Spain, people were still using animal skins as the usual containers for fluids well into the 20th century. (This explains why Spanish wine has only quite recently been seen to have any quality: if you store your wine in an inside-out cowskin, the processes of maturation, while undoubtedly of great interest to the biochemist, are not such as to yield a pleasant potation.) Oak barrels are in fact a lot more ergonomically sophisticated than they look. A hogshead full of wine is too heavy for two strong men to lift, but one slight person can handle it quickly and easily, simply by knowing where to push and when.

Wine casks are an education to the educated. They are products of a craft-based technology which is low on equipment and very high indeed in intelligence and skill. Given an adze and a saw, an oak tree and a few iron bands, *and nothing else*, a skilled cooper could, given time, construct a barrel which would hold water or wine. To most of the people likely to read this book, craft skills such as this are completely alien. In the whole of the developed world, specialisation and machine production have combined to render us unaware of the methods on which our technology is built.

Three hundred years ago, oak trees covered much of the land of western Europe and North America. The genus had mutated to suit local conditions, producing *Quercus robur* and *Q. sessilis* in western Europe and *Q. alba* in the eastern part of north America. (There were lots of other species and sub-species, for *Quercus* mutates very rapidly and easily.) All are eminently suitable for cooperage, in that they bend easily when heated and are stable once cooled. All have high levels of phenolics similar to those occurring naturally in certain wines, though some have more than others: *Q. alba* has about half the level of *Q. robur*, but more than *Q. sessilis*. Thus wine makers seeking a given level of phenolics in their wine may choose from a number of sources.

Trees are cut from the forest. (Recent experience in the USA has shown that naturally seeded forest tress are superior to plantation trees.) They are cut into logs of a suitable length and split longitudinally into four quarters. Each of the four quarters is bandsawn into billets a little larger than the finished stave required for the cask. The wood is then dried, either in kiln or in the air – air-dried staves are superior to kiln-dried because of the flavours they can confer on the wine. Once they are sufficiently seasoned, the billets are sawn and adzed to the typical stave shape: a wide belly tapering to narrower ends, hollowed face and slightly bevelled edges. The staves are then assembled inside two iron hoops, so that all the inner edges mate closely. The inner surface of the wood is wetted and the whole thing is inverted over a roaring fire or a gas burner. The heat softens the wood so much that it is possible, using a steel cable like a garrotte, to draw the open end together sufficiently to allow a hoop to be hammered over it. If the staves have been properly made, each will meet those on either side along the whole of its length. It remains then to inset two end plates, and the barrel will be capable of holding wine, water or any other fluid. The interior of a cooperage is like something out of the Inferno and, to modern eyes, a dangerous and unhealthy place to work. But the frantic activity which normally reigns, and the apparently simple nature of all the tasks, should not blind us to the fact that this is one of the few remaining great craft skills.

We mentioned in earlier chapters how many unlikely things come together to give us our wine. The oak barrel is one of them. Not only can the barrel hold wine, but the chemistry of the oak wood is peculiarly suited to maturing wines. Oak is very high in phenolics that are remarkably similar to those found naturally in some wines. What is more, the oak wood provides a host of flavours and flavour precursors which are peculiarly amenable to the chemistry of improving wine. The process of heating brings about changes in the chemistry of the oak wood which have consequences for the flavour of the wine to be matured in it. By specifying the extent of toasting or charring, the wine maker can exercise some control over the maturation of his or her wines. Toasting produces phenolic and other aldehydes which confer a vanilla flavour, while the degradation of sugars yields toasty aromas. Charring gives the wood a smoky, spicy taste as well as some of the other delicious, spicy flavours such as guaiacol and eugenol.

The extent to which wines are matured in cask varies enormously, being dictated by the nature of the wine; the character which is desired of it, and the extent to which it is capable of benefiting from cask maturation. At one end of the scale are light, aromatic white wines which possess lots of fruity-spicy flavours and very few phenols. Such wines are intended to be drunk very young and no oak flavour is required. They will be filtered and bottled soon after fermentation has ceased and consumed before their delicate flavours have time to diminish. At the other end are the powerful reds which can rest on oak for five years or more before being bottled. The flavours of such wines are so robust that the phenolics and other flavourings extracted from the wood complement and modify the grape and fermentation aromas without overwhelming them, as they would a lesser wine. Then there is every variation in between. Some whites, especially Chardonnays, take happily to long maturation in new oak and can tolerate two years or more without adverse effect. Some reds are bottled without the benefit of any oak at all. Beaujolais Nouveau is an example, which in a good year will be a very pleasing potation despite the absence of oak. Other reds, such as Syrah or Nebbiolo, will take years in oak before they reach a point at which their maker deems them fit for bottling.

We have seen that the variety of wood determines both the type and the intensity of flavourants extracted into the wine. The previous history of the cask matters too: new oak will impart much higher levels of flavour compounds than will oak which has been used previously. Some wine makers prefer the high levels of new oak; others are of the opinion that the softer maturation provided by once- or twice-used casks is more appropriate for their particular wine. Foremost among the extracted flavours are undoubtedly the tannins. Over a year or two, a red wine will remove a large part of the total tannin content of the top few layers of cells of the cask lining. Those tannins will affect the fragrance, taste, mouth-feel and colour of the wine. After tannins, lignin-degradation compounds are the commonest group. The former donate colour and bitter flavours; the latter woody, vanilla aromas. Other wood compounds – and there are hundreds of them – produce caramel and toasted flavours. After a few months, oak lactones may become discernible, from their coconut and berry-fruit flavours. There is a continuous two-way flow in the development of flavour, and oak maturation can dissipate flavour as well as produce it. The green-bean, vegetative flavours so characteristic of Sauvignon Blancs and Cabernet Sauvignons, will often diminish greatly while the wine is in cask, as their components break down and reassemble in the myriad reactions which take place within the walls of a simple wooden barrel.

Maturation is a lengthy business and, as such, ill-suited to the demands of mass-production. Where an oak flavour is required for wine which must be hurried to the market, alternatives exist. Oak chips or shavings can be added to wine in order to give it a flavour of oak. The uptake of flavours is much more rapid than in cask maturation, from the much larger surface area exposed to the wine. Tannins are very much in evidence, as are lactones. Maturation of this sort, though evidently suitable for some wines at the lower end of the market, can hardly be said to be subtle in its end result – but then subtlety is not what that section of the market wants. Those fortunate drinkers who prefer their fine wines should reflect, before deprecating the practice, that if the people who drink the quick stuff all wanted the fine wines, then the prices of the latter would rise very sharply indeed. On the other hand, more of them would be produced in the long run to meet that demand.

BOTTLE-AGEING

One of the pleasures of wine, for folk like me, anyway, is the way in which the one product can bring together the pleasures of craft and science, of tradition and technology. It is a pity that the people who sell wines invariably focus on the craft and tradition and leave out the science and the technology. For in this field as in so many others, the closer one's acquaintance with what is known, the more apparent it becomes that contemporary science is only scratching the surface. A bibliography of recent research in the field of wine flavour runs to hundreds of papers; but even so we still cannot say with any assurance why wine tastes as it does. Some of the main flavour pathways have been identified and hypotheses proposed for some of the main mechanisms, but that is as far as we have got. Science allows the wine maker to exercise a degree of control over the wine-making processes, but at the end of the day, he or she is still standing on the outside, tinkering with externalities, while natural processes take their course.

In no part of the wine making process is this more evident than in the matter of bottle-ageing. You take a quantity of wine, well-made from good grapes, which has lain in oak for an appropriate length of time. It tastes just fine, but you judge that it could be better. You then fill a glass bottle with it, you cork the bottle and you leave the wine in a cool cellar for years. When you open the bottle, provided you have not left it too long, the wine is different and better in all sorts of ways. It is less acidic, less astringent, less citrus-fruity; it feels smoother in the mouth; it tastes of honey, nuts, butter, smoke, etc., and there are fruity flavours of a different sort. The flavours are integrated rather than separate. And all of this has happened with no intervention at all from you: your contribution has been an external one: ensuring that the initial conditions were right; ensuring that there was no variation in the cellar environment. Maybe, if the wine takes a very long time in the cellar, you removed the cork and replaced it with a new one. But that's about all. Science has nothing to do with it. Technology has no place at all. These things happen naturally: all we humans did was to discover *that* they happen, not *how*. We are – or a few of us are – trying to find out how, but at the end of the day there is little need, for it is most unlikely that anyone will find a radically different and better way of making really good wine than the traditional method. Technology may enable us to harvest grapes with a big machine, but we still have to plant vines and grow grapes.

When we think of the application of technology to wines, we tend to think of big New World wineries with stainless-steel vats and pipes and computers controlling everything. But none of that stuff is nearly as important a technological advance as was the simple matter of putting wine in a glass bottle and sealing it in with a cork. It is a long time since anyone other than a wholesaler bought wine by the cask. Indeed most of the main wine-producing countries, aware of the dangers of adulteration and of the added value to be gained from carrying out as much of the production as possible at home, have banned the export of wine except in bottle. When we think of wine, we think of bottled wines. Nevertheless, wine in bottles is a fairly recent arrival on the wine scene. People had been making wine for some thousands of years before anyone thought of putting it in a glass bottle – or at least, before anyone had worked out how to make glass bottles cheaply enough for them to be used for holding wine.

Glass had been known since ancient times and the Romans used the technique of blowing molten glass to form bottles. Bottles may have been used by the Romans for serving wines but, as far as is known, they were not used extensively for keeping wine. The transport vessel at the time was the amphora, which was large and unwieldy, and required to have its contents decanted into a jug or similar container for serving. The use of cork was known in pre-Roman times: the Greeks and the Etruscans used it, coated with resin, to stop the necks of amphorae. (This itself was something of a technological advance on the Egyptians, who had used bunches of reeds for the purpose; one imagines, none too successfully.)

The production in quantity of glass bottles did not become common in Europe until the later 17th century. Around the same time, the use of corks for stopping bottles became common, though it is known that cork had been used to stopper beer bottles for some two hundred years, presumably on a relatively small scale. The 17th-century corks were tapered (unlike today's, which start cylindrical) which allowed them to fit a range of differently sized bottle necks – which was just as well, since the bottles were far from regular. The technology took a great leap forward when, in the 1730s, the production shifted from blown to moulded bottles. It was then possible to make bottles of uniform size and shape, a requirement of industrial-scale production, which came later in the century.

By the fourth decade of the 18th century, the benefits to wine of ageing in bottle came to be recognised, as did the value of laying bottles on their sides to keep the corks wet. Thus was laid the foundation of the great edifice of fine wine. Before then, people had been able to appreciate the difference between good and bad wine, but short of frequenting a reliable source of wine in cask – which being at the end of a long chain of supply, was vulnerable – there was no way of being sure of getting decent stuff. With the advent of cheap cylindrical bottles, it was possible to buy in bulk and lay down wine in cellar with the assurance that not only would it keep, but, within limits, it would improve with time. The same factors of production brought into existence a class of connoisseurs, for whom the appreciation of fine wine was part of the progress of civilisation, in which the 18th century rightly took such pride.

The result was a huge expansion in wine drinking, especially in countries which were not wine producers. The British upper classes had long regarded wine as their natural potation. With the advent of mass-production of bottles and bottled wine of reliable quality, the middle classes also took to drinking wine on a large scale. As the sainted George Saintsbury shows us, it was possible for a Victorian schoolmaster to keep a respectable cellar and to indulge himself in some of the finest vintages. By the second half of the 19th century, the benefits of bottle-age were well appreciated, if little understood. They were to remain little understood for a long time to come. Even today, though some of the larger changes have been identified, the exact nature of many of the processes remains unknown.

Bottle-age can be of benefit to both white and red wines, but it is less common among whites, for fewer white wines improve in bottle than reds. There is a connection between acidity and the ability to age with grace. Wines which when young show little acidity or pronounced flavour are unlikely to improve with age. In wines, as in humans, those which are sharpest when young seem to be the best value when old. The stridency and precociousness which are such an irritant in the young tend to mellow; years take off the sharp edges and in maturity the strong, individual notes of youth are ameliorated to a character which retains variety, but in a more cohesive and appealing form. Acidity as a criterion of the ability to age is suggested by observation of which wines age best: among reds, Cabernet Sauvignon, Syrah and Nebbiolo age better than the likes of Merlot or Pinot Noir. The possession of high levels of phenolics is sometimes suggested as a criterion of the ability to age, but this is contradicted, in the case of white wines at least, by the observation that Riesling and some of the Loire Chenin Blancs, which are low in phenolics, age well, whereas Chardonnay, which is high, on the whole does not.

Acids are instrumental in bringing about the polymerisation of phenolic compounds which is important in both red and white wines. The tannins which cause the bitter taste and the anthocyanins which cause the colour of red wines both form polymers using oxygen (present in either free or bound form, mostly the latter) and acids. Tannin molecules combine with other tannins, with anthocyanins, with salts, with polysaccharides and a whole host of other compounds. Anthocyanins do likewise. There are three consequences of interest to us. Firstly, when two flavour molecules combine with another molecule of the same sort or with something else entirely, there is no guarantee that the new, larger molecule will taste at all like its constituent parts. Indeed there is no guarantee that it will have any flavour at all, as far as we humans are concerned. So the result of the reactions may be (and frequently is) that flavours disappear. In the case of the tannins, it means the wine stops tasting so bitter. Secondly, in the case of anthocyanins, it means the wine changes colour: white wines become yellow, then brown; red wines lose their blue component and their red tends toward brownness. Thirdly, the polymerised phenolic compounds are much larger and therefore heavier than their components, and so are less soluble in the wine. They therefore come out of solution and form sediment in the bottom of the bottle. This sediment is quite different from the sediments formed by tartrates: it is soft and brown whereas the latter are crystalline and take their colour from the wine.

The aroma compounds got from the grape and from the fermentation interact with each other and with phenolics; the fresh, fruity flavours are replaced by other, more complex aromas, in which fruit may be a component, but of a different sort. Acids attached to glucose molecules detach themselves and participate in flavour-producing combinations; aldehydes oxidise to acids and the acids combine with alcohols to form esters, which resurrect some of the fruitiness, or produce a new fruitiness. (This last is hotly disputed, but the balance of opinion seems to be that the esters do play an important part in fruity flavour.)

In ageing as in everything else to do with wine making, it is clear that oxygen is of crucial importance. Oxygen must be excluded from those wines, especially white wines, which are to be bottled immediately after fermentation has ceased, and are intended for drinking young. From fermenter to bottle, the wine must be protected, usually by means of an inert gas such as nitrogen. (Nitrogen isn't really inert, but it is not very reactive and it is a great deal cheaper than any of the true inert gases, argon, neon, etc.) If the wine has access to oxygen, an oxidative bouquet will form in the bottle. While this is acceptable when intentional, such as in fortified wines like sherry and madeira, it produces serious off-odours in non-fortified wines. That said, oxygen is always present in bottled wines, mostly in bound form (i.e. it is incorporated into a compound from which, through enzyme action, it may be released). Many of the reactions which take place during bottle-ageing require oxygen. Since there is no free oxygen (assuming that the cork is tight), the reactions force compounds of which oxygen is a part to release it. When a compound releases its oxygen, the process is called reduction (the opposite of oxidation). Consequently, the bouquet which is formed when wines age in bottle is often referred to as a reductive bouquet. Below threshold levels the reductive bouquet may contribute to overall desirable flavour, but above its very low threshold, reductive bouquet is perceived as an off-odour of sweat, or garlic, or rotten eggs, or cabbage. Organo-sulphur compounds are mainly responsible. They can be released or intensified by bottling and by exposure to light, hence their appellations of 'bottle-stink' and *gout de lumière*. They sometimes can be dispersed by opening the bottle and letting it stand, sometimes by pouring the lot down the drain.

If you are not a chemist, the foregoing may sound as though some folk know a whole lot about it. A very brief review of the literature, however, soon reveals that, though a huge amount of research has been done, flavour-producing mechanisms other than those mentioned are extremely complex and little-understood. And our understanding of ageing in red wines is good, compared to our knowledge of what goes on when you put whites in a bottle. A few things are apparent about the latter. Highly acid wines age better than less-acid ones. Barrel-fermented wines do better than those which have had none. Botrytized wines age well. There are a few more assurances to be got, but not many.

FLAVOUR ORIGINS
≈BAD TASTES≈

We drink wine because it tastes nice, but inevitably some of the wine we drink will taste nasty. Some of the nasty-tasting wine will be unpleasant because it is faulty. In that case, we are entitled to ask for our money back, or for the bottle to be replaced by a good one. But some nasty-tasting wines are unpleasant just because that is how such wines are: they are poorly made, from substandard materials, or bottled without regard to the precautions necessary to avoid spoilage. Most inferior wines are in the lower part of the price range and if you have a bad experience, your only recourse is to avoid buying them again. It is one of the joys of modern wine-drinking that there are lots of cheap wines on the market which are well made from good materials, and are a pleasure to drink. So there is no need to put up with the dross: all that is required is that one remembers the bad wines and avoid them.

The one thing you can't – or shouldn't – do, is to send a cheap wine back because it tastes nasty. On the whole, it is unlikely that the sort of restaurant which will have a sommelier will serve really cheap wines, so the problem of having to argue the case with a waiter much more knowledgeable than yourself will not arise. (Not invariably, but if on the wine list you don't recognise a wildly overpriced inferior wine, you have only yourself to blame.) Most people who have frequented restaurants for many years will have had the experience of ordering a bottle which turns out to be too bad to drink with any pleasure but not bad enough to send back. The only course then is to order another, different one. When doing so, it's worth saying to the waiter that the wine is undrinkable: if the restaurant is any good at all, they will replace it without argument.

Our concern here is not with wines which are bad by nature; it is with wines which ought to be good, but are not because the particular bottle is faulty. When you order a wine which you know to be a good wine, and the bottle which is brought you is off, then you are perfectly entitled to stand on your rights and ask for it to be replaced. And you are justified in making a fuss if it isn't. That's when you ask to see the manager or the owner and threaten to write to the papers. But if you are not to make a complete fool of yourself it's a good idea to know what you are talking about. Most restaurants don't want diners kicking up a row and will acquiesce even if you are in the wrong. But occasionally you may find yourself face to face with a sommelier who really knows his job, who takes a rightful pride in his wines and who will defend a good wine against a bad customer. It's very rare, for managements are on the whole craven in such matters, but happily for the profession of sommelier, it does happen. That's when you have to know your stuff.

There are two circumstances is which you may find yourself condemning a wine: each requires a different tactic. Firstly, there is the situation where you know the wine well. Not only do you know the wine but you know its vintages. If you have a clear mental image of the difference between the 1990 and the 1991, then you are well-equipped to say that what you have been served isn't up to scratch, and to defend your position if you have to. The second circumstance is where you order a wine, of which you do not have previous knowledge, purely on the recommendation of its description in the wine list. In that case, you may reject it only if it is plainly faulty, or if its flavour does not match up to the description.

The subjectivity of flavour sensation means that it is virtually impossible to say that a tasting note is mendacious unless it is wildly out of touch with reality. There are professional tasters of my acquaintance, people of great experience but lacking in scruple, who, because it is in their interest to do so, produce tasting notes which are as florid as they are inaccurate. With the growth of wine tasting as a hobby, the recognition of largely imaginary flavours has become commonplace. It happens mostly among amateurs, but is condoned and practised by a few professionals. There is a great passage in Chapter 10 of Peynaud's *Le Gout du Vin*, which he titles 'Olfactory Analysis Taken To Excess'. He describes a student who, fresh from a wine-tasting course, would give a glass of wine only a cursory inspection before reeling off a long list of flavours which he claimed to have discovered in the wine. Peynaud is very charitable, he does not accuse the student of dishonesty or even of enthusiasm: he merely refers to 'his imaginary garden of smells' into which he invites nobody else.

The issue of a wine's flavours not being what they are said to be is subsidiary to our main concern in this chapter, but it is sufficiently germane for us to look at it briefly. The last ten years have seen a great rise in the use of tasting notes as advertising for the attributes of a wine. The dignified bottles of most wines of quality eschew such parade, relying on their customers' recognition of the label. But the bottles of most mass-marketed wines – which means the vast majority of wines – use tasting notes. The practice is a source of innocent merriment to the knowledgeable, for the disparity between the claimed flavours and those which actually inhere in the wine can be laughably large. So large, indeed, that the public is increasingly sceptical of such claims and their utility as a marketing tool is diminishing.

This is a pity, for only the mendacity of advertisers and the absence of some means of restraining their hyperbole lie between us and a reliable indicator of wine quality. The assessment of flavour is sufficiently well developed for there to be consensus as to which flavours are present in a wine and at what concentration. Such information could be presented on a back label, in the form of a bar chart or even, in outline, of a Flavour Profile. It would require some central authority to authenticate flavour information and some method of policing, but, given the existence of appellation laws in most wine-producing countries, that does not seem altogether impracticable.

It is unlikely we shall have anything of the sort in the foreseeable future. Governments are notoriously slow to act in matters of trade regulation and there are well-placed companies which would stand to lose by it. Only if there were a strong demand from customers would anything be likely to be done. One possibility is to bring a legal case against a wine maker for passing off: for saying that a wine is what it is not. Such a case would require to be well prepared and adequately financed, and it is not clear who might be prepared to mount it. If it were to succeed, though, it could act as a constraint on producers, who would then think twice before putting misleading information on the label of a wine bottle.

Another possibility is that consumers take the matter into their own hands by publicly questioning the veracity of wine-tasting notes, whether in the press, in the wine merchant's or in the restaurant. If enough people take or send a bottle back because it does not taste as it has been said to taste, then shops and restaurants are going to be careful about what wines they stock, for fear of bother. There are precedents for grass-roots social movements of this sort and wine, because so many people feel strongly about it, could conceivably follow them. I hope that the information contained in these pages will be sufficient to enable wine drinkers to form an accurate opinion as to the desirable flavours of a wine. We now turn to the undesirable: the ways in which a wine can be bad: the prima facie reasons for sending it back.

We have seen that making wine involves a surprisingly large number of different operations and that at each stage of its production there are choices to be made between apparently viable alternatives. At each stage the whole thing can go wrong, and going wrong implies producing unpleasant flavours, so there are plenty of opportunities for bad wine. The upside of this is that the greater degree of control over the wine making process exercised by scientific wine makers, means that most of the wines produced in most of the world, are much less likely to be bad than was the case when wine making was still purely traditional.

Wine faults which originate prior to bottling are unlikely to provide cause for complaining about a wine. If the wine is seriously faulty, the wine maker has three choices: to take action to rectify the fault, to bottle the wine under a different label, or not to bottle it at all and sell it for industrial use. We are therefore concerned with faults which either arise in the bottle or are introduced at the bottling stage. Such faults come in a variety of guises and we should admit at the outset that both identification and attribution are highly problematical. Even experienced tasters have problems, not only with saying how the faults came about, but with putting a name to the fault.

CORKS

More people probably know about cork faults than any other faults: indeed, a lot of folk think that whenever a wine smells foul, cork is to blame. This is not the case as we shall see, but there can be no doubt that when a musty, fungal odour is given off by a newly opened bottle the cork is usually responsible. Wines are said to be 'corked' or 'corky' (there is no significance in the different terms) when they have been tainted as a result of flavours derived from the cork. Such flavours take various forms and are attributable to various causes. Wines are not corked when particles of cork are found in the glass. This is caused simply by the disintegration of the cork in being drawn. It can happen to the best of corks drawn by the best of people and it has no flavour significance. The remedy is to remove the bits of cork and get on with drinking the wine.

The most common cause of mouldy cork odours is a compound already mentioned, called 2,4,6-trichloroanisole. (Indeed it is by far the most common cause of all off-odours in wines.) This is an organo-chlorine compound which typically develops in the cork when chlorine is used to bleach it. Almost any contact with chlorine can give rise to the contamination, however; for example, the treatment of the cork oak trees with pentachlorophenol for insect or rot can cause it. There is also a possible pathway which involves bacteria in collusion with pentachlorophenol, though this has not yet been established. It is detectable at very low thresholds indeed: a few parts per trillion will yield a markedly musty odour. Wine which is tainted with 2,4,6-TCA is undrinkable by any but the most desperate of alcoholics and must simply be abandoned.

Mould growth on the cork produces a mouldy aroma. Fungi such as *Penicillium roquefortii* (yes, the stuff that makes the cheese) and various *Streptomyces* bacteria cause the formation of compounds which have a mouldy odour. Other *Streptomyces* species taint cork by metabolising its lignin to produce guaiacol, which has a burned-sugar odour which is rather unpleasant.

Various other off-odours arise from corks. Sulphur contamination can give rise to a musty odour, through the reaction of suphur dioxide with cork lignins to generate thiopyrazines. We won't go into the mechanism by which this happens, for it is complicated, but if a snooty sommelier denies your claim that his wine is corky, or denies that its odour is down to 2,4,6-trichloroanisole, you can hit him with pentachlorophenol and, as a last stop, thiopyrazines.

As a matter of fact, a very common cork fault has nothing at all to do with fancy chemistry. It happens when the cork doesn't fit well enough and allows the ingress of oxygen. The wine will then be oxidised and will show the flat, aldehydic aromas which are the signs of oxidised wine. It is worthwhile to pay attention to the drawing of the cork: a cork of the correct size in good condition should be difficult to draw. If it comes out easily, or if it goes to pieces when the screw is inserted, there is a good chance that it didn't fit properly in the first place, or is rotten, and that air will have got in and wine out. If the whole cork is wet, that is a bad sign, for in a well-fitting cork only the bottom centimetre of cork should be saturated with wine. (In very old bottles, this should not be applied too rigorously, for even the best of corks may deteriorate with great age. Provided the bottle is recorked in time, little harm will be done.)

Various bacteria and yeasts grow on corks and can give rise to off-odours. *Candida* has been known to spoil Champagne and several bacilli are known to produce acrolein in wine, giving it a bitter taint. A last word on corks: there are some grape varieties which have an earthy aroma and you should familiarise yourself with that, and be sure you can tell it from corkiness, before you stick your neck out.

YEASTS AND BACTERIA

As has already been remarked, there are a great many different sorts of yeasts and they are all around us, so at almost any time up until it is bottled wine can be infected with yeasts, often with serious flavour effects. Our concern here is with yeasts which are present in the wine after bottling. Of these, the most serious are members of the *Brettanomyces* genus, which are to be found mainly in red wines. The effects do not show for some six to ten months after bottling, when *B. intermedius* and *B. lambicus* both produce mousy odours. Some *Brettanomyces* also synthesize volatile phenolic compounds to give woody, spicy, horse-manure flavours. The woody and spicy are generally OK but few wine connoisseurs are keen on the aroma of horse-manure in their wine. Other *Brettanomyces* (they are a versatile genus) produce apple aromas and acetic acid.

Musty odours and acetic acid are, however, much more likely to be caused by bacterial action. The best-known genus of acetic acid bacteria is *Acetobacter*, though *Gluconobacter* is just as effective in spoiling wine. The members of the species of both genera will bring about the oxidation of ethanol to acetic acid, but only *Acetobacter* will take it the whole way, given enough oxygen, and break down the acetic acid into water and carbon dioxide. Spoilage can occur at any stage in the production or maturation of the wine, provided there is a source of oxygen. The point at which acetic acid bacteria are most likely to cause contamination which shows up only in the bottle, is in racking. If effective measures are not taken to exclude oxygen or to neutralise it with sulphur dioxide, racking can introduce both the bacteria and the oxygen they require to do their stuff. Then the alcohol in the wine will be oxidised to acetic acid, the acetic acid will react with ethanol to generate ethyl actetate, and the wine will smell of a mixture of vinegar and nail varnish. Very few people can drink anything which smells of vinegar and nail varnish and the only thing to do with the wine is to dump it. The one good thing you can say for acetic acid contamination is that nobody is in any doubt about it, and even the most timid diner can ask for the bottle to be replaced without fear of being snubbed.

After acetic acid bacteria, the most prominent microbial spoilers of wine are various species of *Lactobacillus*. This is the genus that contains the beneficial organisms which bring about the malolactic fermentation by breaking down malic acid to tartaric. Unfortunately some of the species go further and attack the tartaric acid, producing, via one or two intermediaries, acetic acid and carbon dioxide. This is the condition known as *tourne*. Red wines affected by it become dull-red in colour and cloudy, with a viscous sediment. Their flavour is unappealing, mousy, and they may show a slight effervescence. Nobody can be in much doubt and, though the exact cause may not be identified, it will be very apparent that the wine is off. The same bacillus causes another form of spoilage which also has only a French name: *amertume*. This is where the glycerol in the wine is oxidised to form acrolein, which has the bitter taste.

When a wine contains sorbic acid, lactic acid bacteria can bring about a taint which will make the wine undrinkable. The bacteria metabolise the sorbic acid to produce a powerful odour of geraniums. This smell, while it is fine in geraniums, is not desirable in wine. There is no cure except disposal. Again, it is a taint which is easy enough to spot, provided you know what geraniums smell like.

SULPHUROUS ODOURS

Organo-sulphur compounds can be produced at various stages of the life cycle of a wine. Happily, they are very noticeable and unlikely to be allowed into the bottle. However, bottles of wine do sometimes show off-odours which have a sulphur component, especially Champagne and other sparkling wines. This is the condition known as *gout de lumière* and is brought about by exposure to violet and near-ultraviolet light. Amino acids present in the wine are broken down to yield methanethiol and dimethyl disulphide, both of which have pretty nasty smells. What is worse, hydrogen sulphide is generated in the process and adds its moiety to the catalogue of olfactory horrors. Red wines are much less prone to this condition because their tannins bind some of the compounds intermediate in the process. Removal of these contaminants is very difficult and because the process of removing them involves other contaminant substances, the cure may be worse than the disease. Nobody is ever in any doubt as to when organosulphur compounds are present: the smell of rotten eggs is as unmistakable as it is unpalatable.

OXIDATION

We have encountered the deleterious effects of oxygen at various points in the foregoing. It is mostly, but not always, to be avoided. Oxygen is the life-giver and the destroyer. Without it there would be no life as we know it; but it is also what takes away life, for it is inexorable in its actions. We have seen how the process of bottle-ageing requires some oxygen to be present in the wine, in a form in which it is available for the maturation reactions. But if it is present in the free form, its action is prejudicial to the wine, which becomes oxidised. Then white wines will become dull yellow and red wines brown or orange; all will lose their freshness and the fruity character of their aromas, gaining in place of the latter heavy, meaty flavours.

Oxidation is unfortunately still a fairly common fault in wine. It is the worse for often going unrecognised: a mild case may be impossible to detect with certainty unless an unoxidised sample of the same wine is available for purposes of comparison, which happens rarely. Oxidation is progressive, so can occur with varying degrees of severity. Even when the condition is quite pronounced, the drinker may be reluctant to send the bottle back because the evidence is not sufficiently conclusive, oxidised wine being rather similar to some wines whose quality is poor, even if they are not oxidised.

CASSE

This is another French term for which nobody has bothered to devise an exact English equivalent. It refers to metallic solids which precipitate out of solution and form a haze or a sediment, or both. Copper *casse* is a brown cloudiness which tends to disappear as soon as the bottle is opened. The haze is made up of proteins and copper ions. When the bottle is opened and oxygen admitted, the copper ions change from the cuprous to the cupric condition and dissolve, clearing the wine. Iron also forms a *casse*, but usually as sediment. It is caused by iron reacting with phosphates to produce an insoluble compound which is the sediment. It can be cured by fining or by adding citric acid.

PREMATURE DEMISE

In Chapter 8 we saw how some wines have the capacity to age in bottle and some do not; how a great many wines are destined to be bottled as soon as fermentation ceases and to be consumed as quickly as possible thereafter. We then went on, as most writers do, to talk about the wines which age well, and to ask why that was so. There was an assumption implicit in this: that we do not need to say anything more about the cheap wines which are made to be drunk young and whose paltry destiny it may be to make the young drunk.

Few people ask about what happens to such wines when they are not, as intended, consumed when young. Do they simply stay the same? Do they decay? (An honourable exception is David Bird, in *Understanding Wine Technology*.) The answer is that of course they don't stay the same. If we have learned anything about wine, it is that it is never static. No wine stays the same for any length of time, in bottle or out of it. These young wines are subject to the mortality which afflicts all organic products: they lose the bloom of their youth and eventually they fade away. The lively, sharp fruitiness which is their *raison d'être* simply dies away and nothing replaces it. They become pale shadows of what once they were and the smaller the bottle, the quicker the death, for the reactions which cause the effect take place on the interface between the bottle and the wine, and the smaller the bottle, the greater the effect. So if you must buy cheap wines, at least buy big bottles.

TASTING WINES

Now we come to the best bit: the tasting. If you get involved in the subject, it is all too easy to forget that the only thing that really matters about wine is that it tastes nice and that we like drinking it. Appreciating wine is only a means to an end: the enhancement our enjoyment of drinking wines. All that has been said so far in this book, and in every other book about wine, is subsidiary to this end. So now we turn to the consideration of how best to go about putting the knowledge we have gained to use, by tasting a few wines.

There are two ways we can go about tasting wines: we can inspect them dispassionately in circumstances which are as conducive as possible to objective analysis of their flavours, or we can drink them with a view simply to pleasure, but against a background of knowledge such that the pleasure will be maximised. The two approaches are cognate, but sufficiently different that we may legitimately describe them as analytic and synthetic tasting. Analytic tasting maximises our understanding; synthetic tasting, our pleasure. Since the pleasure of appreciation is based on understanding, analytic tasting (up to a point) is the precondition of the pleasure of synthetic tasting. So we will begin with analytic.

ANALYTIC TASTING

The object of all analytic tasting is to discern as accurately as possible the flavours present in a given wine or set of wines. Objectivity is the goal and, to that end, we must arrange things so that every possible cause of bias and every extraneous influence is removed – beginning with the taster.

The flavour of wine is a subjective sensation. It is not too surprising, therefore, that flavour should depend to a great extent on the condition of the person doing the tasting. We are all familiar with the wine which is delicious one day and less than fine the next. The true, the blushful Hippocrene which tastes like rats' piss the morning after is not, objectively, different from what we drank the night before: our perception of it is, though, when conditioned by alcoholic poisoning.

The taster

The most important circumstance of any tasting is the taster. Our perception of flavour is determined by our physiology and our environment: if we wish to be able to assess the flavour of a wine, then the first requirement which must be satisfied is that we, who make the assessment, be in a fit condition. You cannot gauge the brightness of the day, or its temperature, if you have been in a cold, dark place, or if you have a fever. Even if you are well and there seem to be no extraneous circumstances, you cannot be certain of your perceptions, for there may be influences of which you are unaware. This applies, to an extent, to all sense perceptions, for at a fundamental level there can be no certainty of the truth of anything we see, or hear, or smell or taste. The pursuit of certainty has spawned a vast and largely sterile philosophical genre. One thing is sure, even certain: if you wish to pursue that avenue of enquiry, there is enough literature on the subject to last a lifetime. Better to stick to the wine. Our concern is with appreciating wine, and appreciation involves both subjectivity and objectivity. The only certainty we require is that which can be acquired by an ordinary person who is aware that he or she may be wrong. But it helps if we know what things are likely to influence us.

People vary a lot in their ability to taste wines. Some folk have very acute perceptions, others do not. Happily, very few people are so lacking in the basic equipment that they are unable to taste at all and in wine tasting as in almost any other field, one can make do with very limited abilities, provided the will is there. We mentioned early on the condition of anosmia, the inability to smell. If you suffer from that to the extent that you really cannot smell, you are unlikely to have made much sense of this book, so we will dismiss that as a possibility. Much more to the point is the avoidance of activities and conditions which will affect your sense of smell. Suffering from a head cold or similar ailment is an obvious case. Less obvious are various other ailments which affect our sense of smell. There are lots of these – but by the time your nose has gone, you are likely to be so unwell that advising you not to attempt to taste wine is probably superfluous. However, infections of the upper respiratory tract can affect flavour perception long after the infection is over, so you should avoid tasting for some days after any such illness.

Smoking is a disputed area. Most smokers maintain that they are perfectly able to taste wines and anything else, despite their addiction to the weed. In fairness to them, it should be said that the process of adaptation, whereby we accommodate to any uniform background sensation, applies to tobacco smoke as it applies to any other odour. We have already mentioned this phenomenon: there are lots of examples of people being able to taste wines perfectly well against a background of odour. In applying the principle to smoking, however, we should bear in mind that there are more ways than one in which smoking can affect the flavour of wine. Firstly, and most obviously, is the fact that though the smoker may not be affected by the smell of his or her smoke, any non-smokers who are trying to taste wine in the vicinity will be very affected indeed. Secondary smoking may or may not kill you: it sure kills the aromas of a delicate wine. Secondly, even for the smoker, the conditions of tasting are likely to vary so greatly as to render effective flavour detection impossible, unless either he or she does not smoke at all during the tasting and for some considerable time before it. And the inhalation of smoke does long-term harm to the delicate cells of the olfactory epithelium, so that regular smokers are significantly less able to detect aromas than non-smokers.

Personal odours are to be avoided. Not for the sake of the taster, for most people are unaware of their own odour, but for the sake of other tasters. Perfumes should be eschewed – and that goes for deodorants, smelly make-up and male perfumes, even if called by some macho euphemism such as aftershave. Any person intending to taste wine in close proximity to others should consider whether he or she has a detectable personal odour. This is a delicate matter, but one which any conscientious taster ought to address. Everybody smells: to a dog each person has an instantly recognisable odour identity. Most of us don't smell strongly enough to be detectable by the inferior olfactory apparatus of mere humans, but some of us do. Since we all adapt to our own odour, we cannot detect it by ourselves. The only course is to seek outside assistance and ask an honest and courageous friend.

In general, it seems to be best to taste before meals rather than after, for it is then that one's olfactory abilities are at their most acute, though one research project has shown that our ability to detect aromas actually increases after eating. It may be that people are different in this, so it is worth trying both to see which suits you. Certainly it is not a good idea to try to taste wines after a *heavy* meal.

If you are a woman, you have an inbuilt advantage when it comes to tasting wine, for various studies have shown that women are more acute than men in the detection of aromas, and more skilled in identifying them. Some of this may be cultural, for in the developed world women have more contact with aromas than men do. Besides perfumes as such, most cosmetics are perfumed and women constantly make choices between different odours. But nothing is for nothing, and your advantage comes at a price. If you are between puberty and menopause, your ability to detect and identify odours will vary with your hormonal condition. There isn't much you can do about this, except learn to deal with it.

We now come to possibly the most important cause of taster-induced variation: the taster's state of mind. What we taste depends to a great extent on us: on our attitudes and our beliefs, our experience and our intentions. It also depends on our personality: remember Peynaud's story of the taster who learned the flavours by rote and had no doubt that he discerned them all in a glass of wine, though he had hardly put his nose in it. That sort of tasting is no good to anybody – and of course it is shown up the instant the taster tries to taste blind, for, lacking the name of the wine, he is at a loss to identify the flavours. If your tasting is to be any good at all, to yourself or to anybody else, it is essential that you keep an open mind, as free as possible from extraneous influence, and that you rely solely on your own perceptions.

This is harder than it seems. It is especially difficult to admit that you fail to detect an aroma, when you are assured that it is present. None of us likes to seem incompetent in anything we do, but in tasting wine there is an added layer of difficulty. We have seen how the signals from the nose make connections in the brain which are closely involved with our emotional responses. This makes us peculiarly open to persuasion in the matter of odours. I spent years conducting tutored tastings – not of wine, but of whisky, but the principle is the same – in which I would lead a group of enthusiasts through a series of glasses, describing the flavours of each. That sort of thing gets boring after a while, so one day, just as an experiment, I described a flavour in one glass which I knew was not present. Every taster claimed to discern the flavour and some went so far as to describe it in detail. Curious, I did the same thing several times. On one occasion, several of the tasters went so far as to discuss the nuances of a flavour which was purely imaginary. I then – as an experiment and in the interest of science, you understand – went even further and conducted tastings in which, in every glass tasted, I said I detected a flavour which manifestly was not present. I did it several times. In some of the tastings, every student said he or she could taste every imaginary flavour. In some of the tastings, a few of the students said they had difficulty in detecting the fake flavours, but never a majority of the students and never all of the flavours.

And it's not just enthusiasts: Peynaud tells of a group of expert tasters who were comparing wines which had been heat-treated with the same wines which had not. After they had tasted a few and found the relevant differences, Peynaud gave them two identical wines. Each taster then discerned a difference, although the two wines had come out of the one bottle. So professionals may be just as gullible as amateurs. Indeed, professionals are under more pressure to conform than amateurs are, since their livelihood depends on their olfactory abilities. One suspects that this conformity is behind the fashions which from time to time afflict the wine world. If a wine, or a style of wine, becomes fashionable, then lots of people say they like it and buy it; because it sells well, there is commercial pressure in its favour. It takes a stout heart to stand out against the consensus which this creates. Happily for us all, the wine business is blessed with a few excellent critics – the Jancis Robinsons and the Oz Clarkes of this world – who can be discerned, like rocks standing above the foam, washed by the waves of fashion but rarely submerged.

So where, dear reader, does this leave you? How do you free yourself from influence, and attain to the Olympian heights of pure, unsullied perception of the flavours which actually exist in a wine? We shall come in a moment to the mechanics which you must get right if you are to have the best chance of discovering aroma, bouquet and taste. But before you attend to those, you must seek to free your mind, to attend only to your own sensations, and to distinguish between what you actually taste and what you only think you taste. It isn't easy, especially if until now you have been unused to doing anything of the sort. But it is a skill like other skills, and you get better at it if you practise. While we are about it, we should look briefly at the notion of skill, for wine tasting is a skill and skills are little valued or understood in the modern world. We have said a lot about science in this book but, so far, nothing about skills. It's a big subject, but I will try to put it briefly.

Our knowledge about the world, and particularly our knowledge about how to do things, is of two main sorts. Science is one of them. It is the sort of knowledge which is most characteristic of our society: a highly structured way of getting and developing our knowledge which has clear rules and is subject to empirical testing (which is what experiments are about). Science as it exists today is by far the most successful set of methods ever devised for learning about the world. And it works: the reason why only the feeble-minded believe in stuff like astrology is that astrology doesn't approximate to reality – it doesn't work. More than two thousand years ago, the Greeks ditched astrology in favour of an approach which today we would call scientific. This is a classic comparison: between science and a non-scientific way of knowing. But there has always been another way of knowing, which is hugely important and which has received very little notice from the philosophers, namely the acquisition and exercise of skills.

Skill-based learning is mainly a way of learning how to do things. It differs from scientific knowledge in that in science all the data and the theories are made explicit. In a science textbook the assumptions and hypotheses are laid out as clearly as possible, and the closeness of their correspondence with reality examined systematically. (This is what scientific experiments do.) With skill-based learning, nothing is explicit. It is a way of acquiring knowledge without anything being spelt out. Typically, we learn a skill by *doing*. Until the Industrial Revolution, almost all knowledge apart from philosophy and religion (and they weren't worth much, with a few honourable exceptions) was skill-based. All production of goods was by skilled craftsmen. The mystery of a craft was exactly that: mysterious. It consisted of a body of knowledge which the possessors could make explicit only by doing what they did, for there was no language which could describe it. There still isn't, for the most part. The acquisition of a skill is predicated on a huge quantity of information about how and how not to do things. Every time we carry out a skilled action, that database is subconsciously called into play. We all have skills, if sometimes not very refined ones. Driving a car is a very skilled business. So is knitting. So is making mayonnaise. Most sports require the acquisition and exercise of skill and we learn how to be good at sports in the way which typifies skills: by practice. And a lot of science depends on skill: there are lots of experiments which require a skilled experimenter to get the right (i.e. the scientific) result. If all this seems a bit obscure, and remote from tasting wine, let me give you an example.

Many years ago, when I was in my late teens, I was working on the deck of a ship. We were stowing a large piece of cargo and the ship's carpenter was directing. There was need for a piece of timber of a certain size, and the carpenter, who was enormous, grabbed a great baulk of timber, laid it across his knee, and sawed it through. None of that is too surprising: what astonished me was the saw cut the carpenter made. It was perfectly regular and exactly at right angles to the timber. I was astonished because for years I had tried to make straight saw cuts and had always failed miserably, despite having more conducive conditions than a beam across my knee. It was many years before I was to gain some understanding, which I did as follows. Firstly, I learned how to saw a straight line. I guess it's something you could make rules about, but that's not how people learn such things. You learn to saw wood by sawing wood, and doing it badly, and reflecting on what you have done, and trying again in the light of your reflection, and keeping doing that until you can saw a straight line. It can take years. Secondly, I was lucky enough to have a friend who was a skilled craftsman, and who understood what he was doing. Berty was apprenticed as a cabinet-maker in Bohemia in the late 1930s. Having a practical skill saved his life, for he was taken from Auschwitz, where he had been incarcerated, to eastern Poland, as a slave labourer for the Nazis. Berty later became an internationally famous architect and town planner. He was a scholar and a gentleman who never lost his delight in making things out of wood. He told me that when he began his apprenticeship, his first six months were spent solely in sharpening tools. It was he who introduced me to the basics of urban transport planning and who showed me how to put a razor edge on a chisel – no mean skill in itself. We often talked about philosophy and carpentry, and I owe him what little understanding I have of how we get to know about the world by doing things well.

Tasting wine is no less a skill than designing cities or playing golf. Where tasting wine differs from golf is that golf has an explicit criterion of success (getting the ball into a little hole) and tasting wine does not. Nobody who isn't an idiot expects to be able to walk onto a golf course and do as well as a professional, but lots of folk think that they can taste wine effectively, simply by supping a few glasses of the stuff. They think this because tasting wine is a skill, and the database of a skill is, by definition, invisible. The purpose of the second part of this book is to help you acquire the taster's skill. The object of the first part of the book was to equip you with as much relevant information as possible, for tasting, like any skill, requires a knowledge base. You learn to taste by practice and by criticism. Unless you are fortunate enough to study with a master, you must be your own critic. This is the hardest way to learn, but in some ways the best, for by being your own critic, you learn a discipline which may be lacking in them as is 'larned' in schools – vide Peynaud's student. You must constantly ask yourself whether you do really smell what you think you smell: you must pay attention to your sensations. It isn't easy and the hardest part of it is the criticism. You mustn't expect it to be quick. If there is one thing all skills have in common, it is that they take time to acquire. And once you have it, you must keep in practice, for some skills are lost much more easily than they are gained. Others, like riding a bike, you don't lose, but some you do, and smelling is, alas, one of the latter. I have a friend who is a professional perfumer. Every morning in his lab before he starts work, his assistant lays out for him about twenty perfume samples. He has to identify them all. He says that if he doesn't do that, his perspicuity declines rapidly.

The tasting environment

For analytic tasting, the environment should be as odour-free as possible. It is a good idea to inspect the tasting room before the commencement of any tasting – and to ensure that you lock it afterwards. (I once set up an elaborate tasting, laid out glasses, etc, the night before the session, only to find in the morning that the cleaning lady had been in and had polished the table with a furniture polish perfumed with synthetic lavender. The place stank. The tasting had to be aborted and all the glasses washed.) The location of the tasting room matters, too, for smells may drift in from outside. I remember attending a tasting of Portuguese wine in a room above an Indian restaurant. It was not a success, to put it mildly. Air conditioning can help, but only if it is good air conditioning, for systems vary a lot and some do no more than draw air from the street and cool it, so you get air-conditioned aromas from whatever restaurant is nearby. Natural air is by far the best, preferably not in a city and, unhappily, not close to a garden, for the scents of flowers can be just as prejudicial as those of curry. I expect a sandy desert would be ideal if the humidity could be improved.

A tasting room should be at a comfortable temperature and moderate humidity. It should be adequately lit, preferably by natural light. Some people make a fuss about lighting, for they think the colour of a wine matters a lot. I can't say I agree: at the end of the day, all that matters about a wine is its flavour. Colour is important only as an indicator of flavour – and in a strictly controlled tasting the colour ought not to be evident, so as to leave the assessment of flavour as free from influence as possible. The use of dark tasting glasses is not common, though obscuring the colour of the wine is at least as important a precaution against bias as is hiding the bottle label and shape. Cobalt glass is perfect: not only does the blue glass look great, but blue is the only colour which carries almost no associations with food or drink. This, however, is for purists.

Apropos glasses: wine should preferably be pre-poured, so that tasters do not see the shape of the bottle. It is common to hide labels, and this is OK provided the bottles are all of the same sort. Otherwise, decant or pour individual glasses where the tasters cannot see them. If glasses are to be poured more than a few moments before they are tasted, they should be covered to prevent the evaporation of the more volatile flavour components. The best cover is a watch glass, but anything will do, provided it prevents the escape of gas and is itself perfectly flavour-free.

Where two or more people are to taste wines simultaneously, they should be isolated from each other as far as possible, so as to prevent any cross-influence. If isolation is not possible, it may be desirable to have them taste the wines in different order.

The instructions given to the tasters depend on the purpose of the tasting. In a general tasting, it is usual to ask tasters to comment on sweetness, acidity, bitterness, aroma, off-notes, body, colour and general appearance. Normally, some sort of score card is issued, which lists the aspects of the wine which it is desired the tasters should comment on or rate. For grading purposes, a zero score on any head indicates poor quality, one ordinary and two good. The most-used card is one devised at the Enology department of the University of California at Davis. It is, however, intended to cover attributes other than flavour as well as flavour information, and was devised to allow comparison of young wines with a view to their improvement, so is a little beside our purpose.

The method I propose is to use a grid which will convert readily into a Flavour Profile, as follows.

The wines are to be rated on a scale of zero to ten for the presence of flavours which fall into the principal aroma categories of the Aroma Wheel (see page 27), plus the three taste categories of sweet, acid and bitter. Obviously, the problem with this system is to give the tasters a standard for comparison, so that they may know how strong each flavour requires to be to score a ten or a five or any other rating. If only a comparative tasting is required, tasters need only be asked to adopt some subjective measure, but if an absolute rating is wanted, some objective criterion is necessary. This can fairly easily be provided by means of a set of standard wines. An anonymous wine possessing as little character as possible is taken as a base and is spiked with flavour components. Tasters are asked to taste the standards as examples of ten-scores, with the original wine as a zero-score on all counts. All the wines tasted are then measured against the standards. It is not a perfectly accurate method, but probably an improvement on what has gone before. Once all the scores are collected, they require to be analysed. Strictly speaking, this is a matter for a statistician, though many quite sophisticated statistical analyses are available as computer programmes, so that running one is not as daunting an affair as once it was.

The equipment

The first piece of kit you need is, obviously, glasses. You need plenty of them: one per wine per taster, with a few spare, for nosing glasses (as they are called) have an irritating habit of getting themselves broken. Good glasses are absolutely essential: a glass must give you room for the wine, room to swirl it round without losing lots, and a mouth narrow enough to retain volatile aromas without being so narrow that you get a sore neck because you have to tilt back so far to drink from the glass. (This is a problem with sherry copitas.)

A lot of work has gone into the design of wine glasses. The technology of glass drinking was developed in the 18th and 19th centuries, roughly parallel with that of bottle-making. (There was some fine glassware before that, but it was such a luxury article that it had no impact on wine-drinking habits.) Glasses played an important part in the rise of the middle-class connoisseurship which was the economic base of the expansion of the wine industry in the 19th and 20th centuries. English lead crystal was the first glassware to be made to standards which would be regarded as adequate today. Its introduction at the end of the 18th century set a standard for wine glasses which was not reached by mass-production methods until the second half of the 20th century.

Today it is possible to buy cheaply glassware which is perfectly adequate in every sense. There can be no doubt that a fine glass enhances the pleasure of drinking a wine, as does a white linen tablecloth or a table top of well-polished mahogany. The expansion of the wine market has led to a proliferation of glass styles, each supposedly suited to a particular wine. Naturally, the manufacturers of glasses are very keen on this, and the wine magazines reluctant to rubbish it, for fear of lost advertising revenue. Most of it is nonsense. There have been numerous reports of supposedly objective assessments of the flavour-enhancing qualities of particular glasses for particular wines. I have not read one which has obeyed the most elementary principle of blind tasting: namely that the tasters should be perfectly ignorant of the identity of what is tasted. If it is the glass which is being tested then the same goes for the glass. Naturally, blind tasting is a lot more difficult with wine glasses than it is with wines, for it is very difficult to hide the glass without preventing its being used. Nonetheless, it remains that the results of such tests are deeply suspect.

The glass used in the trade and generally reckoned to be about as good as it gets for discerning aroma is the ISO (International Organization for Standardization) standard tasting glass. This was designed around 1970 by some French expert wine tasters. It was based on research carried out by the INAO (L'Institut National des Appellations d'Origine). It is cheap to produce, of a pleasing appearance, and it does its job as well as anyone could wish.

The tastevin, which is a sort of cup with a handle used in some wine caves for tasting wines from the cask, is the traditional tasting tool in many parts of Europe. It has the sanction of tradition, but that is about all it has going for it: it is quite useless for assessing aroma and if anyone has memories of the fine savour of wine taken from a tastevin in a cave in Burgundy, he or she should question whether the aromas were due to the tastevin, or to the atmosphere of the cave itself. If there is any question, it is an easy one to put to the test: get yourself a tastevin, or any kitchen vessel which approximates to it in shape and size, and try it out against an ISO glass. Then you will see the difference, irrespective of the sort of wine.

If wine is to be tasted seriously, it is necessary to provide a spittoon for each taster. Best is a sink with running water, as in a laboratory, or the little sinks dentists use which swirl water round and down a central hole. Failing that, provide a jug or carafe for each taster. The jug should always be opaque: there are few sights less conducive to an appreciation of the aesthetic qualities of a fine wine than a jar half-full of murky, viscous spit.

If the tasting room is to accommodate a lot of people tasting a lot of wines, and the circumstances permit, you can't do much better than boxes of sawdust for spittoons. It looks right and it is easy to dispose of. Only be careful as to the sawdust, for if you get it from a sawyer who just happens to have cut a load of pitch-pine, it can easily scent the whole room. And don't think old sawdust will do better: the stuff loses its aroma quite quickly if you let it stand, but only on the surface, so that if it is stirred up, it will again emit a remarkably strong aroma. Oak won't do either, for the tannic odours it releases will confuse the wine aromas. Whitewood sawdust is best.

Most spitting nowadays is done into small vessels, for the good reason that few people have the expertise necessary to spit accurately into a vessel on the floor. I recall the first professional wine tasting I ever attended, as the guest of a lady who was wine critic to one of the big Sunday newspapers. I thought the tasting was just fine and was on my best behaviour. After it, I asked whether I had passed muster and was told that all the folk were most impressed. I couldn't think of anything that might have impressed them and was surprised when she told me that it was my spitting. Apparently the casual, accurate expectoration at a trajectory into a spittoon some distance away, was viewed with respect and some envy. I explained that I had gone to the sort of school at which spitting was *de rigeur*, and besides I had heredity on by side – both my father (who smoked black plug) and my grandfather (who chewed tobacco) having been accurate and elegant spitters.

Decanters will be needed for old wines. You may get by with a basket which holds the bottle nearly horizontal, but it is risky, and you are unlikely to wish to risk old and proportionately expensive wine, so decant in advance. Leave the bottle with the decanter, with its cork attached to the neck by a rubber band. The ideal in any blind tasting (and remember, no analytic tasting which isn't blind is worth a damn) is for the tasters not to see the bottles at all. If you have the premises, a separate booth should be provided for each taster, so that he or she is completely isolated. If that can't be achieved, next best is to pour the wines out of sight of the tasters and serve them in glasses. If the wine bottles have to be in view, then the simplest course is to wrap each in a sheet of paper, with a numeral on each sheet for identification. (An A4 sheet goes nicely round most wine bottles. Stick it in place with some Sellotape or the like.)

Stationery and pens or pencils should be provided for any tasting. The organiser of the tasting will determine the nature of the stationery. It normally takes the form of cards or papers which are arranged so that the taster can rate the wines according to the organisers' requirements. (See above.) Bottles should be clearly identified and their markings should correspond with the tasting sheets. Arrangements should be made for collection of the sheets as soon as the tasters have completed them. (If they are left on the table they are likely to get stained and soggy.) If tasters are to be standing, a surface or a clipboard should be provided; if a clipboard, it is a good idea to attach a pencil to it by a string. White napkins are desirable but rarely provided. Linen is by far the best, as regards both appearance and its tactile qualities. Take care the napkins have no odour.

Procedure

When arranging a tasting, thought should be given to the order in which the wines are presented. Ideally, each of the tasters should get the wines in a different order for, as you should know by now, how something tastes depends to a great extent on what was tasted just before it. In randomising the order of tasting wines, however, thought should be given to what the results of the random selection will be. No order should be adopted solely because it is different if it means that a delicate, pale Pinot Gris will follow a big red Hermitage. Indeed, it is best to group wines as closely as possible in terms of their presumed flavours: red with red and white with white; tough, country reds together with their rustic cousins and not alongside refined wines from the Côte-d'Or, for the comparison will be of value in respect of neither and the flavour of one may well interfere with that of the other.

Flavour interference is difficult to avoid if very different wines are to be tasted in the same session. So is olfactory fatigue. Our noses get tired just as do any other of our faculties. If you are sniffing similar sorts of things for any length of time, olfactory adaptation will occur, and the scent will diminish in apparent strength. The cure for this is very simple, but for some reason is little-mentioned or practised among wine tasters. Have to hand a big jug of tap water. Good, scentless tap water, that is: if your tap water has any smell at all, use a good bottled water, but not a spa water. When your nose becomes tired, sniff the jug of water several times. Sniff it good and hard. The water will cleanse the olfactory epithelium of whatever is adhering to it, and you will find your perception of aromas wonderfully restored. Besides being handy at any time when nosing, this is useful for countering flavour interference. If you sniff the water jug after any particularly strong wine, its effects will rapidly diminish. Since it takes only a few seconds, there really is no reason why you shouldn't sniff water after every wine.

It is always useful to have in front of one a list of the possible aromas. We all have the disturbing experience of recognising a smell but being unable to identify it. If you have the Aroma Wheel list handy, perhaps padded out with a few of Peynaud's additional aroma terms, the field should be pretty-well covered. If you then find a distinct odour you can't recognise, at least the field will be narrowed to things not on the list.

Having made your preparations, it remains only to apply yourself to the wine. If it is a halfway decent wine, 90 percent of the interest is going to come from the nose, so it is with that instrument that you must firstly address the wine. If there is a watch glass over the glass, remove it and have a sniff. There is little point in sniffing while thinking of something else: you must be perfectly concentrated on the aroma of the wine. Only later, when you are expert, may you become blasé, and nose a wine accurately while talking about last night's football match. As an apprentice, you must be totally concentrated on the task. It's all a bit Buddhic, really: the clearing of the mind, the cleansing of the senses and the perfect receptivity. And if you find you don't smell much, or don't smell the things you are told the wine smells of, remember what we said about skills: this is a skill which you must learn, and you learn it only by trying and failing and trying again, many times, until you begin to catch the merest glimmer of what you are looking for. And if some sophisticate condescends to you because you are struggling, well, that's what that sort of person does. It doesn't make you any less. If the admission of ignorance is the first step on the road to understanding, you can reflect that they have yet to take the first step – and if they don't change their ways, they maybe never will.

When addressing the wine, you should remember that the most volatile aromas will come off first, so you must try to catch those and identify them. You are more likely to catch them in flight by quick sniffs than by deep breathing in the glass. And you must trust to first impressions, for that is all you may get. You sniff the wine, a word pops into your mind: write it down; don't stop to examine whether you are right or wrong. Critical examination of one's perceptions is both logically and temporally posterior to the perceptions themselves. The main thing is to register those first impressions. To do that, you must not be afraid of making a fool of yourself. I mentioned earlier my first experience of a professional wine tasting. It was at that tasting that I drank my first-ever glass of really top-quality champagne. My lady friend asked me what it smelt of and I said, 'Biscuits' – truthfully, for it smelt like those horrible little sweet biscuits with coloured cream sandwiched between sugary shortcrust which my granny always kept in a little barrel. I thought I had really blown my credibility, but it turned out that I had said exactly the right thing and that classy Champagne really does smell of biscuits: vulgar, fancy biscuits.

The wine reveals itself over time. Or good wine does, anyway: simple wine is like simple minds: what you see is what you get. But for depth, you need two things: the effect of volatility on the wine and the effect of habituation on the taster. As the more volatile aromas strip away, the underlying flavours will reveal themselves. You just keep it up until there isn't any more development. Mostly that won't take long, though in the case of a really great wine it can occupy you for the best part of an evening.

Once you have a handle on the nose, taste the stuff. You will then experience two sorts of sensation: you will taste it, obviously, but you will also experience the aroma, as the flavour components travel via the retronasal passages to the olfactory epithelium. There will be no more leisurely discriminating bouquet: everything happens at once and you are called on to discriminate among the different sensations and to decide the levels of each you perceive. This is analytic tasting and it's a lot harder than just saying you think the stuff is nice and rounded and has fine tannins and isn't quite as wholesome as the '84.

If you are tasting correctly and strictly analytically, that's a end on it. You spit it out and move onto the next one.

SYNTHETIC TASTING

The phrase 'synthetic tasting' came about firstly as an obvious antonym to 'analytic tasting'. It seemed like a convincingly fancy name for something which wanted one: the business of tasting intelligently but without the limitations imposed by rigorously scientific approach. Also, it had echoes of the Hegelian dialectic, which seemed a good thing. (If you haven't heard of the Hegelian dialectic, there is a good chance you will be impressed, for it sounds suitably Germanic and philosophical. If you are one in a million and *have* heard of it, you are likely to be even more impressed, for though you won't have read it, you will know that it's about as incomprehensible as philosophy gets. If you have read it and you aren't one of the six people on the planet who seem to understand it, then with any luck you may think I'm one of those six people. If you are one of the six people, you are unlikely to condescend to read a book about mere wine.)

The idea of synthesis is of putting things together rather than taking them apart. Synthetic tasting is the sort of thing people can do who have done their homework and can take a wine to pieces and inspect the bits, but choose not to do so. Then when they taste a wine, and enjoy it, they do so against a background of knowledge which increases their enjoyment but does so without intruding. All the analysis – which the whole of this book has been about – is for professionals who require it for their jobs or for nerds who have nothing better to do – unless it can be employed to enhance our enjoyment of our wine. I could give a hundred examples. It's like the people watching a sailing boat: one sees only the spectacle and says, 'Isn't it lovely?' The other sees exactly the same thing and says, 'It is, but he wants to sheet his main in harder, or come off the wind a bit.' The latter understands how to sail a boat and knows the helmsman hasn't got it quite right, so while he likes the scene no less, he *appreciates* it more, for he understand what is going on. Or the musician who, hearing Jimi Hendrix play a riff on the guitar, knows how it's fingered but also knows he will never, if he practises for a thousand years, get it to sound like that. He hears the same sound as you or I, but his hearing is tinged with wry knowledge, and he can truly be said to appreciate what he hears, in a way that you and I do not. That's what appreciating wine is about. I'm not saying my appreciation of wine is in that class, but all knowledge helps us to appreciate, and we can all appreciate to the best of our ability. It's not a race: there are no winners and losers, but there can be no doubt that the more you learn about wine, the more you come to appreciate it. We will now turn to a few appreciations.

APPRECIATIONS

JOH. JOS. PRUM RIESLING 1995

From the French–German border, the Mosel runs in a northeasterly direction to meet the Rhine at Koblenz. About halfway down, the river takes a bend to the left and heads in a northwesterly direction. On the right bank, which faces southwest, there is steep slope which looks across to the village of Wehlen on the other side of the river. The most famous vineyard on the slope is the Sonnenuhr, which takes its name from a huge sundial cut into the rock. The sundial stands out white against the background of vines. The latter are brown in winter, green in summer and they grow Riesling grapes, some of which are vinified by the Prum family, which has been making wine at Wehlen for a very long time. When, in the early 1980s, the rest of Germany was going for quantity at any cost, the Prums disdained such temporary pursuits and continued to produce wines of great depth and concentration, made with Riesling grapes grown on low-yielding vines.

The Riesling grape will grow in northern climes such as Germany, but it will yield its best only on south-facing slopes such as those of the Sonnenuhr. There it concentrates the flavour compounds derived from the schists (rocks) beneath to produce a wine of great elegance and strength.

This wine shows the Riesling at its most intense. The first impression is of the sulphurous odours so often found in the very best Riesling wines. The stuff smells like a rubber tyre factory: so much so that some of our tasters are deterred and wish to go no further. But they do, and are gratified that they do, for the wine proceeds to reveal fruit and flowers, which simply overwhelm the malodorous sensations. There is sweetness too, and enough acidity to

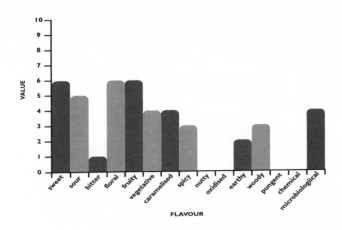

act as a counterweight. More of one or the other and the whole thing would have been a lesser wine – but the balancing act of the bouquet is maintained in the taste. It is apparent that this is a very fine wine indeed, which will be even better in ten years, and in twenty and, who knows, for a long time after that.

DRY RIVER SAUVIGNON BLANC 2001

We have heard a lot about how some grapes suit particular places: the complex of attributes and influences which combine to produce a unique *terroir*. Daft though it seems, one is tempted to make a case for extending the notion of *terroir* to include the culture of the place. If that were to be true of anywhere, it would be true of New Zealand, where the land and the climate come together with a young, energetic, scientifically literate community of wine makers to produce wines of a peculiar excellence. It is a combination which seems to suit Sauvignon Blanc particularly well.

This happy conjunction first came to the notice of the northern hemisphere in the wines from New Zealand's South Island, led by Cloudy Bay. However, in recent years Neil McCallum's Dry River Sauvignon Blanc from the North Island has laid claim to the top position, certainly in New Zealand, and perhaps in the whole of the New World.

The wine assails the nose with the characteristic Sauvignon Blanc vegetative aromas: grassy, green and fresh as a well-watered garden ground. Flowers grow in that garden, lots of flowers, of lots of different types. Fruit grows there too – melons, peaches, lychees and

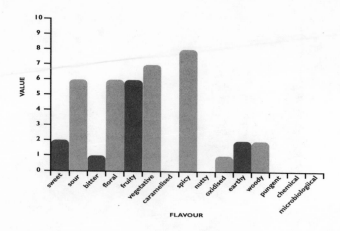

passion fruit. As you delve, there is just a whiff of earth and wood, but nothing to detract from the fruit and the flowers. There is a sharp acidity which quite overwhelms any residual sugars. This is not a wine for drinking by its own – but none the worse for that. Take it with meat or cheese or any other food which will act as a foil for the acidity and you will have an experience well worth the little effort it will cost you.

ORLANDO JACOB'S CREEK CHARDONNAY

We should get things in their proper scale before looking at the wine which follows. The J.J. Prum wine on page 180 comes from a vineyard which extends to some 36 acres, from which in a good year they get 120,000 bottles. The Puligny Montrachet, below, is from one which is even smaller. The Orlando winery in Rowland Flat, Barossa Valley, which makes the Jacob's Creek Chardonnay, is 4,940 acres in extent. In addition to the grapes from that vineyard, the winery uses grapes brought in by refrigerated road tanker, some from far afield. Its total annual output of wine is about a hundred million bottles. These are sold all over the world and are especially popular in the United Kingdom.

There is no talk here of *terroir*, for this is industrial production on the largest scale. The company, appropriately, is very large and is owned by the huge Pernod-Ricard conglomerate. Orlando wines are a bit like Ford cars: they are looked down on by folk who can afford to buy the much more expensive article, but Orlando have used the

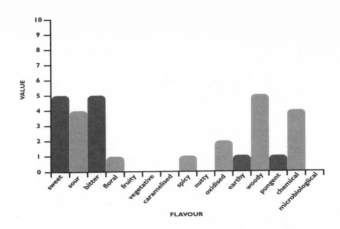

technology to produce an artefact which is very efficient at doing what it is intended that it should do. And like Ford cars, millions of people around the world are very grateful that something so cheap should do its job so well.

This is a wine which is emphatically for drinking. It has little to offer the nose, and indeed it is better not to linger too long, for there are some odours in the Chemical category which will show if you persist. But treat it right, drink it, and you will find acidity nicely moderated by sweetness and enough tannins to make it oaky and moreish.

PULIGNY MONTRACHET LES DEMOISELLES 1991

One of the joys of wine is its sheer variety. A lot of people moan about the industrialisation of wine production, and about the increasing dominance of a few grape varieties. The scale of production which allows us to have decent wines very cheaply also allows us to save our cash to splash out occasionally on something really fine and individual. The Montrachet appellation lies on the Côte de Beaune, a few kilometres south of the town of Beaune. It straddles the boundaries of two villages: Chassagne and Puligny. You could lose the whole lot in a corner of the Orlando vineyard. Madame François Colin bottles a small quantity of very fine white wine under the designation of Puligny-Montrachet Les Demoiselles.

There are two things to be said of this. Firstly, it is rated as a

Premier Cru, which is deemed to be slightly less worthy than a Grand Cru, and secondly, it is made from the same Chardonnay grape as the Jacob's Creek. As regards the Cru status, we should keep things in proportion. The white Burgundies are rated by a lot of people as just about the best wines in the world. The difference between Premier Cru and Grand Cru is one which may be apparent to some folk in Beaune, but I doubt if one wine drinker in a million could find a difference as regards the quality of the wine. There is variety, yes, for each wine is individual, despite (or possibly because of) the tiny holdings. The astonishing thing is that such stuff should be made from this grape, which is the same varietal as produced the Jacob's Creek. Look at the Flavour Profile: it shows a larger number of hits in the flavour categories than any of the wines we have seen so far. There are all sorts of things there.

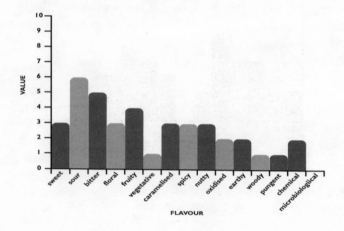

It is very dry, but the tannins serve to balance the acidity. So does the alcohol, which at 13.5 per cent is substantial. There are floral and fruity aromas, with spice and nuts and woodiness, as befits the grape variety and the use of wood. There is also that whiff of sulphur which is enough to emphasise, but not enough to diminish, the deliciousness of the whole. What the Flavour Profile can't show is the variety, and the cohesion of the whole lot into something just wonderful. You wouldn't necessarily want to drink it all the time (nonsense, says the alter ego: you would scoff that every day if you got the chance) but it is great stuff for a celebration or a sneaky indulgence.

BRUNELLO DI MONTALCINO LISINI 1995

In the hills to the south of the lovely renaissance town of Siena lies the Lisini family estate. It has 25 acres of vineyards whose soil is a mixture of stones and clay, all planted with the Sangiovese clone known as Brunello. This grape has small berries with very thick skins. The skins contribute a disproportionately high level of phenolics to the must and the resultant wine (unblended, unlike so much Italian wine) is full-flavoured and robust. It is aged in wood for at least five years, during which time it picks up so much additional tannin from the wood that when young the wine is excessively bitter.

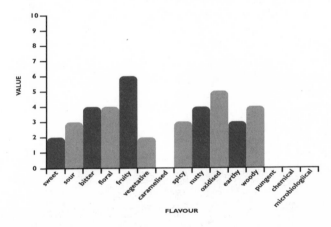

But the same tannins allow it to age indefinitely in bottle. Then the phenols soften and transmute into high levels of the most perfectly delicious flavours: fruity, with the deep, flavoursome fruit of maturity. The wine is delicious now, at six years old, but it will benefit from another generation or so in cellar. With that concentration of phenols, it is capable of retaining both structure and flavour until very old indeed.

VIEUX CHATEAU CERTAN POMEROL 1997

Pomerol is a relative newcomer (by French standards) to the world of first-rate wines. It was for long completely overshadowed by the great wines of the region. In the last half-century, however, the wines of Pomerol have found a place alongside the very finest that money can buy – and money can buy you some very fine wines indeed. There are no appellations in Pomerol, but the place is not so large that one

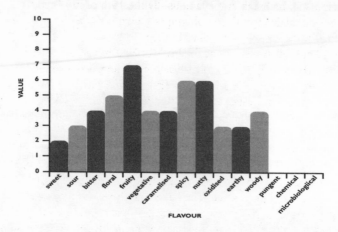

cannot soon learn which châteaux are capable of what. The Vieux Château Certan is capable of producing some of the finest wines of Pomerol: lovely, dense, deeply flavoured wines which are drinkable at five years old, but will last as long as you will.

This is the land where Merlot is king. Some Pomerols use pure Merlot; others blend in a little Cabernet Franc and some, like Vieux Château Certan, use Cabernet Sauvignon as well. The result is spectacular: not in any strident and easily identifiable character, but in the integrated flavours of what is undoubtedly a great wine. The wine is now five years old and just coming into its own. The tannic flavours of its youth have muted into soft, floral aromas against a background of berry fruits. There are nutty, spicy flavours as well and enough of the earth for the wine to put one in mind of the soil it sprang from, despite its undoubted elegance. This is alchemy: the base metals of the soil are transmuted into something more valuable than mere gold.

HERMITAGE JEAN-LOUIS CHAVE, 1987

A bit south of the town of Vienne, the Rhône takes a sharp turn to the left, to run for a little while almost due east. This means that the left bank faces south and it is on that south-facing bank that the hill of Hermitage lies. The hill is of granite, covered by a thin soil which varies from place to place. The whole hill is of no great size, which severely limits the amount of wine which may be called Hermitage, for only wine made from grapes grown on the hill may bear the famous name. The black grapes are all Syrah: indeed this is the place which made the Syrah grape famous. By the 19th century red Hermitage made from the Syrah grapes grown on the hillside were among the most expensive wines in the world.

Jean-Louis Chave owns small parcels of land in various parts of the hill, on which he grows the blue-black Syrah grapes which are blended to make a wine which may truly claim to represent the best of Hermitage. The grapes are harvested by hand and hot-fermented in a very traditional manner. Maturation is in oak casks, which adds phenolics to the already tannic wine. The result is a wine which will age almost indefinitely, becoming softer and deeper as it does.

Our example is now fifteen years in bottle and is just about right for drinking. The tannins have diminished in intensity, though they are still a powerful presence. The flavour of the wine is rich and spicy, with overtones of fruit and nuts. There are woody, earthy flavours as well and a sulphurous note which adds to the impression of richness without detracting in the least. The only problem one has with a wine like this is the thought that, if it is left, it may be even better in ten or twenty years. However, intimations of one's own mortality suggest that maybe it's more than good enough now. Much as I like old wines, I don't intend to have any deathbed regrets about the wines I might have drunk, but didn't, so we open another bottle.

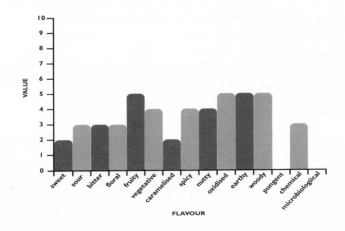

INDEX